MICROWAVE

COOKBOOK 2022

QUICK AND DELICIOUS RECIPES FOR SMART PEOPLE

JANE BENNETT

Table of Contents

Fruit and Nut Butter Cheesecake... 13

Preserved Ginger Cake.. 14

Preserved Ginger Cake with Orange... 15

Honey Cake with Nuts... 16

Gingered Honey Cake.. 18

Gingered Syrup Cake... 19

Traditional Gingerbread... 19

Orange Gingerbread.. 21

Coffee Apricot Torte 21

Rum Pineapple Torte 22

Rich Christmas Cake 23

Fast Simnel Cake 25

Seed Cake... 26

Simple Fruit Cake 28

Date and Walnut Cake... 29

Carrot Cake 30

Parsnip Cake... 31

Cheese Fondue.. 32

Fondue with Cider 33

Fondue with Apple Juice... 33

Pink Fondue.. 33

Smoky Fondue... 34

German Beer Fondue... 34

Fondue with Fire 34

Curried Fondue.. 34

Fonduta... 35

Mock Cheese and Tomato Fondue.. 35

Mock Cheese and Celery Fondue... 36

Italian Cheese, Cream and Egg Fondue....................................... 37

Dutch Farmhouse Fondue 38

Farmhouse Fondue with a Kick.. 39

Baked Egg Flamenco Style 40

Bread and Butter Cheese and Parsley Pudding 41

Bread and Butter Cheese and Parsley Pudding with Cashew Nuts 42

Four-cheese Bread and Butter Pudding.. 42

Cheese and Egg Crumpets... 43

Upside-down Cheese and Tomato Pudding................................... 44

Pizza Crumpets 45

Gingered Sea Bass with Onions... 46

Trout Packets 47

Shining Monkfish with Slender Beans 48

Shining Prawns with Mangetout.. 49

Normandy Cod with Cider and Calvados..................................... 50

Fish Paella... 52

Soused Herrings... 54

Moules Marinières 55

Mackerel with Rhubarb and Raisin Sauce................................... 57

Herring with Apple Cider Sauce.. 58

Carp in Jellied Sauce... 59

Rollmops with Apricots 60

Poached Kipper 61

Prawns Madras 62

Martini Plaice Rolls with Sauce 63

Shellfish Ragout with Walnuts 65

Cod Hot-pot 67

Smoked Cod Hot-pot 68

Monkfish in Golden Lemon Cream Sauce 68

Sole in Golden Lemon Cream Sauce 70

Salmon Hollandaise 70

Salmon Hollandaise with Coriander 71

Salmon Mayonnaise Flake 72

Mediterranean-style Salmon Roast 73

Kedgeree with Curry 74

Kedgeree with Smoked Salmon 75

Smoked Fish Quiche 76

Louisiana Prawn Gumbo 77

Monkfish Gumbo 78

Mixed Fish Gumbo 78

Trout with Almonds 79

Prawns Provençale 80

Plaice in Celery Sauce with Toasted Almonds 81

Fillets in Tomato Sauce with Marjoram 82

Fillets in Mushroom Sauce with Watercress 82

Hashed Cod with Poached Eggs 83

Haddock and Vegetables in Cider Sauce 85

Seaside Pie 86

Smoky Fish Toppers 88

Coley Fillets with Leek and Lemon Marmalade 89

Seafish in a Jacket 90

Swedish Cod with Melted Butter and Egg 91

Seafood Stroganoff 92

Fresh Tuna Stroganoff 93

White Fish Ragout Supreme 93

Salmon Mousse 95

Dieters' Salmon Mousse 97

Crab Mornay 97

Tuna Mornay 98

Red Salmon Mornay 98

Seafood and Walnut Combo 99

Salmon Ring with Dill 101

Mixed Fish Ring with Parsley 102

Cod Casserole with Bacon and Tomatoes 103

Slimmers' Fish Pot 104

Roast Chicken 106

Glazed Roast Chicken 107

Tex-Mex Chicken 108

Coronation Chicken 109

Chicken Veronique 110

Chicken in Vinegar Sauce with Tarragon 111

Danish Roast Chicken with Parsley Stuffing 112

Chicken Simla 112

Spicy Chicken with Coconut and Coriander 113

Spicy Rabbit 114

Spicy Turkey 114

Chicken Bredie with Tomatoes 115

Chinese Red Cooked Chicken 116

Aristocratic Chicken Wings 117

Chicken Chow Mein 118

Chicken Chop Suey 119

Express Marinaded Chinese Chicken 119

Hong Kong Chicken with Mixed Vegetables and Bean Sprouts ... 120

Chicken with Golden Dragon Sauce 121

Ginger Chicken Wings with Lettuce 122

Bangkok Coconut Chicken 123

Chicken Satay 124

Peanut Chicken 125

Indian Chicken with Yoghurt 126

Japanese Chicken with Eggs 127

Portuguese Chicken Casserole 128

English-style Spicy Chicken Casserole 129

Compromise Tandoori Chicken 129

Pumpkin Cake 131

Scandinavian Cardamom Cake 132

Fruited Tea Bread 134

Victoria Sandwich Cake 135

Walnut Cake 136

Carob Cake 137

Easy Chocolate Cake 137

Almond Cake 137

Victoria Sandwich Gâteau 138

Nursery Tea Sponge Cake.. 139

Lemon Sponge Cake... 140

Orange Sponge Cake 140

Espresso Coffee Cake 141

Orange-iced Espresso Coffee Cake 142

Espresso Coffee Cream Torte.. 142

Raisin Cup Cakes... 143

Coconut Cup Cakes 144

Chocolate Chip Cakes 144

Banana Spice Cake 145

Banana Spice Cake with Pineapple Icing........................... 146

Butter Cream Icing 146

Chocolate Fudge Frosting.. 147

Fruited Health Wedges 148

Fruited Health Wedges with Apricots.................................. 149

Shortbread 149

Extra Crunchy Shortbread.. 150

Extra Smooth Shortbread... 150

Spicy Shortbread.. 150

Dutch-style Shortbread... 150

Cinnamon Balls.. 151

Golden Brandy Snaps 152

Chocolate Brandy Snaps.. 153

Bun Scones... 154

Raisin Bun Scones.. 155

Breads 155

Basic White Bread Dough.. 156

Basic Brown Bread Dough *157*

Basic Milk Bread Dough *157*

Bap Loaf *158*

Bap Rolls *158*

Hamburger Buns *159*

Fruited Sweet Bap Rolls *159*

Cornish Splits *159*

Fancy Rolls *160*

Rolls with Toppings *160*

Caraway Seed Bread *161*

Rye Bread *161*

Oil Bread *162*

Italian Bread *162*

Spanish Bread *162*

Tikka Masala Bread *163*

Fruited Malt Bread *164*

Irish Soda Bread *166*

Soda Bread with Bran *167*

To Freshen Stale Bread *167*

Greek Pittas *167*

Jellied Cherries in Port *168*

Jellied Cherries in Cider *169*

Mulled Pineapple *170*

Mulled Sharon Fruit *171*

Mulled Peaches *171*

Pink Pears *172*

Christmas Pudding *173*

Butter Plum Pudding *174*

Plum Pudding with Oil *174*

Fruit Soufflé in Glasses *175*

Almost Instant Christmas Pudding *176*

Ultra-fruity Christmas Pudding *178*

Plum Crumble *179*

Plum and Apple Crumble *180*

Apricot Crumble *180*

Berry Fruit Crumble with Almonds *180*

Pear and Rhubarb Crumble *180*

Nectarine and Blueberry Crumble *181*

Apple Betty *182*

Nectarine or Peach Betty *182*

Middle Eastern Shred Pudding with Nuts *183*

Cocktail of Summer Fruits *184*

Middle Eastern Date and Banana Compôte *185*

Mixed Dried Fruit Salad *186*

Stodgy Apple and Blackberry Pudding *187*

Lemony Bramble Pudding *188*

Lemony Raspberry Pudding *189*

Apricot and Walnut Upside-down Pudding *190*

Bananas Foster *192*

Mississippi Spice Pie *193*

Jamaica Pudding *195*

Pumpkin Pie *196*

Oaten Syrup Tart *198*

Coconut Sponge Flan *199*

Easy Bakewell Tart *200*

Crumbly Mincemeat Pie *201*

Bread and Butter Pudding *203*

Lemon Curd Bread and Butter Pudding *204*

Baked Egg Custard *205*

Semolina Pudding *206*

Ground Rice Pudding *206*

Steamed Suet Treacle Pudding *207*

Marmalade or Honey Pudding *207*

Ginger Pudding *208*

Jam Sponge Pudding *208*

Lemon Sponge Pudding *209*

Crêpes Suzette *210*

Baked Apples *211*

Thousand Petal Haddock with Crab *212*

Lemon and Thyme Cod *213*

The Good Wife's Cod *214*

French-style Cod *215*

Manhattan Cod *216*

Curried Cod with Coconut *217*

Fish Vinaigrette *218*

Jugged Kipper *218*

Fruit and Nut Butter Cheesecake

Serves 8–10

A continental-style cheesecake, the sort you'd find in a quality patisserie.

45 ml/3 tbsp flaked (slivered) almonds
75 g/3 oz/2/3 cup butter
175 g/6 oz/1½ cups oaten biscuit (cookie) or digestive biscuit (Graham cracker) crumbs
450 g/1 lb/2 cups curd (smooth cottage) cheese, at kitchen temperature
125 g/4 oz/½ cup caster (superfine) sugar
15 ml/1 tbsp cornflour (cornstarch)
3 eggs, at kitchen temperature, beaten
Juice of ½ fresh lime or lemon
30 ml/2 tbsp raisins

Put the almonds on a plate and toast, uncovered, on Full for 2–3 minutes. Melt the butter, uncovered, on Defrost for 2–2½ minutes. Thoroughly butter a 20 cm/8 in diameter dish and cover the base and side with the biscuit crumbs. Beat the cheese with all the remaining ingredients and stir in the almonds and melted butter. Spread evenly over the biscuit crumbs and cover loosely with kitchen paper. Cook on Defrost for 24 minutes, turning the dish four times. Remove from the microwave and leave to cool. Chill for at least 6 hours before cutting.

Preserved Ginger Cake

Serves 8

225 g/8 oz/2 cups self-raising (self-rising) flour
10 ml/2 tsp mixed (apple-pie) spice
125 g/4 oz/½ cup butter or margarine, at kitchen temperature
125 g/4 oz/½ cup light soft brown sugar
100 g/4 oz/1 cup chopped preserved ginger in syrup
2 eggs, beaten
75 ml/5 tbsp cold milk
Icing (confectioners') sugar, for dusting

Closely line a 20 cm/8 in diameter soufflé or similar straight-sided dish with clingfilm (plastic wrap), allowing it to hang very slightly over the edge. Sift the flour and spice into a bowl. Finely rub in the butter or margarine. Fork in the sugar and ginger, making sure they are evenly distributed. Stir to a soft consistency with the eggs and milk. When smoothly combined, spoon into the prepared dish and cover lightly with kitchen paper. Cook on Full for 6½–7½ minutes until the cake is well risen and beginning to shrink away from the side. Allow to stand for 15 minutes. Transfer to a wire rack by holding the clingfilm. Peel away the wrap when cold and store the cake in an airtight container. Dust with icing sugar before serving.

Serves 8

Prepare as for Preserved Ginger Cake, but add the coarsely grated peel of 1 small orange with the eggs and milk.

Honey Cake with Nuts

Serves 8–10

A star of a cake, full of sweetness and light. It is Greek in origin, where it is known as karithopitta. Serve it with coffee at the end of a meal.

For the base:

100 g/3½ oz/½ cup butter, at kitchen temperature

175 g/6 oz/¾ cup light soft brown sugar

4 eggs, at kitchen temperature

5 ml/1 tsp vanilla essence (extract)

10 ml/2 tsp bicarbonate of soda (baking soda)

10 ml/2 tsp baking powder

5 ml/1 tsp ground cinnamon

75 g/3 oz/¾ cup plain (all-purpose) flour

75 g/3 oz/¾ cup cornflour (cornstarch)

100 g/3½ oz/1 cup flaked (slivered) almonds

For the syrup:

200 ml/7 fl oz/scant 1 cup warm water

60 ml/4 tbsp dark soft brown sugar

5 cm/2 in piece cinnamon stick

5 ml/1 tsp lemon juice

150 g/5 oz/2/3 cup clear dark honey

For decoration:

60 ml/4 tbsp chopped mixed nuts
30 ml/2 tbsp clear dark honey

To make the base, closely line the base and side of an 18 cm/7 in diameter soufflé dish with clingfilm (plastic wrap), allowing it to hang very slightly over the edge. Put all the ingredients except the almonds in a food processor bowl and run the machine until smooth and evenly combined. Pulse in the almonds briefly to stop them breaking up too much. Spread the mixture into the prepared dish and cover lightly with kitchen paper. Cook on Full for 8 minutes, turning the dish twice, until the cake has risen appreciably and the top is peppered with small air pockets. Allow to stand for 5 minutes, then invert into a shallow serving dish and peel away the clingfilm.

To make the syrup, place all the ingredients in a jug and cook, uncovered, on Full for 5–6 minutes or until the mixture just begins to bubble. Watch closely in case it starts to boil over. Allow to stand for 2 minutes, then gently stir round with a wooden spoon to mix the ingredients smoothly. Spoon slowly over the cake until all the liquid is absorbed. Combine the nuts and honey in small dish. Warm through, uncovered, on Full for 1½ minutes. Spread or spoon over the top of the cake.

Gingered Honey Cake

Serves 10–12

45 ml/3 tbsp orange marmalade

225 g/8 oz/1 cup clear dark honey

2 eggs

125 ml/4 fl oz/½ cup corn or sunflower oil

150 ml/¼ pt/2/3 cup warm water

250 g/9 oz/generous 2 cups self-raising (self-rising) flour

5 ml/1 tsp bicarbonate of soda (baking soda)

3 tsp ground ginger

10 ml/2 tsp ground allspice

5 ml/1 tsp ground cinnamon

Closely line a deep 1.75 litre/3 pt/7½ cup soufflé dish with clingfilm (plastic wrap), allowing it to hang very slightly over the edge. Put the marmalade, honey, eggs, oil and water in a food processor and blend until smooth, then switch off. Sift together all the remaining ingredients and spoon into the processor bowl. Run the machine until the mixture is well combined. Spoon into the prepared dish and cover lightly with kitchen paper. Cook on Full for 10–10½ minutes until the cake is well risen and the top is covered with tiny air holes. Allow to cool almost completely in the dish, then transfer to a wire rack by holding the clingfilm. Carefully peel away the clingfilm and leave until completely cold. Store in an airtight container for 1 day before cutting.

Gingered Syrup Cake

Serves 10–12

Prepare as for Gingered Honey Cake, but substitute golden (light corn) syrup for the honey.

Traditional Gingerbread

Serves 8–10

A winter's tale of the best kind, essential for Hallowe'en and Guy Fawkes night.

175 g/6 oz/1½ cups plain (all-purpose) flour
15 ml/1 tbsp ground ginger
5 ml/1 tsp ground allspice
10 ml/2 tsp bicarbonate of soda (baking soda)
125 g/4 oz/1/3 cup golden (light corn) syrup
25 ml/1½ tbsp black treacle (molasses)
30 ml/2 tbsp dark soft brown sugar
45 ml/3 tbsp lard or white cooking fat (shortening)
1 large egg, beaten
60 ml/4 tbsp cold milk

Closely line the base and side of a 15 cm/6 in diameter soufflé dish with clingfilm (plastic wrap), allowing it to hang very slightly over the edge. Sift the flour, ginger, allspice and bicarbonate of soda into a mixing bowl. Put the syrup, treacle, sugar and fat in another bowl and heat, uncovered, on Full for 2½–3 minutes until the fat has just melted.

Stir well to blend. Mix with a fork into the dry ingredients with the egg and milk. When well combined, transfer to the prepared dish and cover lightly with kitchen paper. Cook on Full for 3–4 minutes until the gingerbread is well risen with a hint of a shine across the top. Allow to stand 10 minutes. Transfer to a wire rack by holding the clingfilm. Peel away the clingfilm and store the gingerbread in an airtight container for 1–2 days before cutting.

Orange Gingerbread

Serves 8–10

Prepare as for Traditional Gingerbread, but add the finely grated peel of 1 small orange with the egg and milk.

Coffee Apricot Torte

Serves 8

4 digestive biscuits (Graham crackers), finely crushed
225 g/8 oz/1 cup butter or margarine, at kitchen temperature
225 g/8 oz/1 cup dark soft brown sugar
4 eggs, at kitchen temperature
225 g/8 oz/2 cups self-raising (self-rising) flour
75 ml/5 tbsp coffee and chicory essence (extract)
425 g/14 oz/1 large can apricot halves, drained
300 ml/½ pt/1¼ cups double (heavy) cream
90 ml/6 tbsp flaked (slivered) almonds, toasted

Brush two shallow 20 cm/8 inch diameter dishes with melted butter, then line the bases and sides with the biscuit crumbs. Cream together the butter or margarine and sugar until light and fluffy. Beat in the eggs one at a time, adding 15 ml/1 tbsp flour with each. Fold in the remaining flour alternately with 45 ml/3 tbsp of the coffee essence. Spread equally into the prepared dishes and cover loosely with kitchen paper. Cook, one at a time, on Full for 5 minutes. Allow to cool in the dishes for 5 minutes, then invert on to a wire rack. Chop three of the apricots and set aside the remainder. Whip the cream with the remaining coffee essence until thick. Take out about a quarter of the cream and stir in the chopped apricots. Use to sandwich the cakes together. Cover the top and sides with the remaining cream. Press the almonds against the side and decorate the top with the reserved apricots, cut sides down.

Rum Pineapple Torte

Serves 8

Prepare as for Coffee Apricot Torte, but omit the apricots. Flavour the cream with 30 ml/2 tbsp dark rum instead of the coffee essence (extract). Stir 2 chopped canned pineapple rings into three-quarters of the cream and use to sandwich the cakes together. Cover the top and sides with the remaining cream and decorate with halved pineapple rings. Stud with green and yellow glacé (candied) cherries, if wished.

Rich Christmas Cake

Makes 1 large family cake

A luxurious cake, full of the splendours of Christmas and well endowed with alcohol. Keep it plain or coat it with marzipan (almond paste) and white icing (frosting).

200 ml/7 fl oz/scant 1 cup sweet sherry
75 ml/5 tbsp brandy
5 ml/1 tsp mixed (apple-pie) spice
5 ml/1 tsp vanilla essence (extract)
10 ml/2 tsp dark soft brown sugar
350 g/12 oz/2 cups mixed dried fruit (fruit cake mix)
15 ml/1 tbsp chopped mixed peel
15 ml/1 tbsp red glacé (candied) cherries
50 g/2 oz/1/3 cup dried apricots
50 g/2 oz/1/3 cup chopped dates
Finely grated peel of 1 small orange
50 g/2 oz/½ cup chopped walnuts
125 g/4 oz/½ cup unsalted (sweet) butter, melted
175 g/6 oz/¾ cup dark soft brown sugar
125 g/4 oz/1 cup self-raising (self-rising) flour
3 small eggs

Put the sherry and brandy in a large mixing bowl. Cover with a plate and cook on Full for 3–4 minutes until the mixture just begins to bubble. Add the spice, vanilla, the 10 ml/2 tsp brown sugar, the dried fruit, mixed peel, cherries, apricots, dates, orange peel and walnuts. Mix thoroughly. Cover with a plate and warm through on Defrost for 15 minutes, stirring four times. Leave overnight for the flavours to mature. Closely line a 20 cm/8 in diameter soufflé dish with clingfilm (plastic wrap), allowing it to hang very slightly over the edge. Stir the butter, brown sugar, flour and eggs into the cake mixture. Spoon into the prepared dish and cover loosely with kitchen paper. Cook on Defrost for 30 minutes, turning four times. Allow to stand in the microwave for 10 minutes. Cool to lukewarm, then carefully transfer to a wire rack by holding the clingfilm. Peel away the clingfilm when the cake is cold. To store, wrap in a double thickness of greaseproof (waxed) paper, then wrap again in foil. Store in a cool place for about 2 weeks before covering and icing.

Fast Simnel Cake

Makes 1 large family cake

Follow the recipe for Rich Christmas Cake and store for 2 weeks. The day before serving, cut the cake in half to make two layers. Brush both cut sides with melted apricot jam (conserve) and sandwich together with 225–300 g/8–11 oz marzipan (almond paste) rolled out to a thick round. Decorate the top with shop-bought miniature Easter eggs and chicks.

Seed Cake

Serves 8

A reminder of old times, known in Wales as shearing cake.

225 g/8 oz/2 cups self-raising (self-rising) flour
125 g/4 oz/½ cup butter or margarine
175 g/6 oz/¾ cup light soft brown sugar
Finely grated peel of 1 lemon
10–20 ml/2–4 tsp caraway seeds
10 ml/2 tsp grated nutmeg
2 eggs, beaten
150 ml/¼ pt/2/3 cup cold milk
75 ml/5 tbsp icing (confectioners') sugar, sifted
10–15 ml/2–3 tsp lemon juice

Closely line the base and side of a 20 cm/8 in diameter soufflé dish with clingfilm (plastic wrap), allowing it to hang very slightly over the edge. Sift the flour into a bowl and rub in the butter or margarine. Add the brown sugar, lemon peel, caraway seeds and nutmeg and mix in the eggs and milk with a fork to form a smooth, fairly soft batter. Transfer to the prepared dish and cover loosely with kitchen paper. Cook on Full for 7–8 minutes, turning the dish twice until the cake has risen to the top of the dish and the surface is peppered with small holes. Allow to stand for 6 minutes, then invert on to a wire rack. When completely cold, peel away the clingfilm, then turn the cake the right way up. Combine the icing sugar and lemon juice to make a thickish paste. Spread over the top of the cake.

Simple Fruit Cake

Serves 8

225 g/8 oz/2 cups self-raising (self-rising) flour
10 ml/2 tsp mixed (apple-pie) spice
125 g/4 oz/½ cup butter or margarine
125 g/4 oz/½ cup light soft brown sugar
175 g/6 oz/1 cup mixed dried fruit (fruit cake mix)
2 eggs
75 ml/5 tbsp cold milk
75 ml/5 tbsp icing (confectioners') sugar

Closely line an 18 cm/7 in diameter soufflé dish with clingfilm (plastic wrap), allowing it to hang very slightly over the edge. Sift the flour and spice into a bowl and rub in the butter or margarine. Add the sugar and dried fruit. Beat together the eggs and milk and pour into the dry ingredients, stirring to a smooth soft consistency with a fork. Spoon into the prepared dish and cover loosely with kitchen paper. Cook on Full for 6½–7 minutes until the cake is well risen and just beginning to shrink away from the side of the dish. Remove from the microwave and allow to stand for 10 minutes. Transfer to a wire rack by holding the clingfilm. When completely cold, peel away the clingfilm and dust the top with sifted icing sugar.

Date and Walnut Cake

Serves 8

Prepare as for Simple Fruit Cake, but substitute a mixture of chopped dates and walnuts for the dried fruit.

Carrot Cake

Serves 8

Once called paradise cake, this transatlantic import has been with us for a good many years and never loses its appeal.

For the cake:
3–4 carrots, cut into chunks
50 g/2 oz/½ cup walnut pieces
50 g/2 oz/½ cup packeted chopped dates, rolled in sugar
175 g/6 oz/¾ cup light soft brown sugar
2 large eggs, at kitchen temperature
175 ml/6 fl oz/¾ cup sunflower oil
5 ml/1 tsp vanilla essence (extract)
30 ml/2 tbsp cold milk
150 g/5 oz/1¼ cups plain (all-purpose) flour
5 ml/1 tsp baking powder
4 ml/¾ tsp bicarbonate of soda (baking soda)
5 ml/1 tsp mixed (apple-pie) spice

For the cream cheese frosting:
175 g/6 oz/¾ cup full-fat cream cheese, at kitchen temperature
5 ml/1 tsp vanilla essence (extract)
75 g/3 oz/½ cup icing (confectioners') sugar, sifted
15 ml/1 tbsp freshly squeezed lemon juice

To make the cake, brush a 20 cm/8 in diameter microwave ring mould with oil and line the base with non-stick parchment paper. Put the carrots and walnut pieces into a blender or food processor and run the machine until both are coarsely chopped. Transfer to a bowl and work in the dates, sugar, eggs, oil, vanilla essence and milk. Sift together the dry ingredients, then stir into the carrot mixture with a fork. Transfer to the prepared mould. Cover with clingfilm (plastic wrap) and slit it twice to allow steam to escape. Cook on Full for 6 minutes, turning three times. Allow to stand for 15 minutes, then turn out on to a wire rack. Remove the paper. Invert on to a plate when cooled completely.

To make the cream cheese frosting, beat the cheese until smooth. Add the rest of the ingredients and beat lightly until smooth. Spread thickly over the top of the cake.

Parsnip Cake

Serves 8

Prepare as for Carrot Cake, but substitute 3 small parsnips for the carrots.

Cheese Fondue

Born in Switzerland, Cheese Fondue is the après-ski darling of Alpine resorts or anywhere else with deep snow on high peaks. Dipping your bread into a communal pot of aromatic melted cheese is one of the most convivial, entertaining and relaxing ways of enjoying a meal with friends and there is no better kitchen helper for this than the microwave. Serve with small tots of Kirsch and cups of hot lemon tea for an authentic atmosphere.

1–2 garlic cloves, peeled and halved
175 g/6 oz/1½ cups Emmental cheese, grated
450 g/1 lb/4 cups Gruyère (Swiss) cheese, grated
15 ml/1 tbsp cornflour (cornstarch)
300 ml/½ pt/1¼ cups Mosel wine
5 ml/1 tsp lemon juice
30 ml/2 tbsp Kirsch
Salt and freshly ground black pepper
Cubed French bread, for dipping

Press the cut sides of the garlic halves against the sides of a deep 2.5 litre/4½ pt/11 cup glass or pottery dish. Alternatively, for a stronger taste, crush the garlic directly into the dish. Add both cheeses, the cornflour, wine and lemon juice. Cook, uncovered, on Full for 7–9 minutes, stirring four times, until the fondue begins to bubble gently.

Remove from the microwave and mix in the Kirsch. Season well to taste. Bring the dish to the table and eat by spearing a cube of bread on to a long fondue fork, swirling it round in the cheese mixture, then lifting it out.

Fondue with Cider

Serves 6

Prepare as for Cheese Fondue, but substitute dry cider for the wine and calvados for the Kirsch and serve cubes of red-skinned apple as well as the bread cubes for dipping.

Fondue with Apple Juice

Serves 6

A non-alcoholic Fondue with a mellow taste and suitable for all ages.

Prepare as for Cheese Fondue, but substitute apple juice for the wine and omit the Kirsch. If necessary, thin down with a little hot water.

Pink Fondue

Serves 6

Prepare as for Cheese Fondue, but substitute 200 g/7 oz/1¾ cups each white Cheshire cheese, Lancashire cheese and Caerphilly cheese for the Emmental and Gruyère (Swiss) cheeses and rosé wine for the white wine.

Smoky Fondue

Serves 6

Prepare as for Cheese Fondue, but substitute 200 g/7 oz/1¾ cups smoked cheese for half the Gruyère (Swiss) cheese. The quantity of Emmental cheese is unchanged.

German Beer Fondue

Serves 6

Prepare as for Cheese Fondue, but substitute beer for the wine and brandy for the Kirsch.

Fondue with Fire

Serves 6

Prepare as for Cheese Fondue, but add 2–3 red chillies, seeded and very finely chopped, just after the cornflour (cornstarch).

Curried Fondue

Serves 6

Prepare as for Cheese Fondue, but add 10–15 ml/2–3 tsp mild curry paste with the cheeses and substitute vodka for the Kirsch. Use pieces of warmed Indian bread for dipping.

Fonduta

Serves 4–6

An Italian version of Cheese Fondue, inordinately luscious.

Prepare as for Cheese Fondue, but substitute Italian Fontina cheese for the Gruyère (Swiss) and Emmental cheeses, dry white Italian wine for the Mosel, and marsala for the Kirsch.

Mock Cheese and Tomato Fondue

Serves 4–6

225 g/8 oz/2 cups mature Cheddar cheese, grated
125 g/4 oz/1 cup Lancashire or Wensleydale cheese, crumbled
300 ml/10 fl oz/1 can condensed tomato soup
10 ml/2 tsp Worcestershire sauce
A dash of hot pepper sauce
45 ml/3 tbsp dry sherry
Warmed ciabatta bread, to serve

Place all the ingredients except the sherry in a 1.25 litre/2¼ pt/5½ cup glass or pottery dish. Cook, uncovered, on Defrost for 7–9 minutes, stirring three or four times, until the fondue is smoothly thickened. Remove from the microwave and stir in the sherry. Eat with pieces of warm ciabatta bread.

Mock Cheese and Celery Fondue

Serves 4–6

Prepare as for Mock Cheese and Tomato Fondue, but substitute condensed celery soup for the tomato soup and flavour with gin instead of sherry.

Italian Cheese, Cream and Egg Fondue

Serves 4–6

1 garlic clove, crushed

50 g/2 oz/¼ cup unsalted (sweet) butter, at kitchen temperature

450 g/1 lb/4 cups Fontina cheese, grated

60 ml/4 tbsp cornflour (cornstarch)

300 ml/½ pt/1¼ cups milk

2.5 ml/½ tsp grated nutmeg

Salt and freshly ground black pepper

150 ml/¼ pt/2/3 cup whipping cream

2 eggs, beaten

Cubed Italian bread, to serve

Place the garlic, butter, cheese, cornflour, milk and nutmeg in a deep 2.5 litre/4½ pt/11 cup glass or pottery dish. Season to taste. Cook, uncovered, on Full for 7–9 minutes, stirring four times, until the fondue begins to bubble gently. Remove from the microwave and mix in the cream. Cook, uncovered, on Full for 1 minute. Remove from the microwave and gradually beat in the eggs. Serve with Italian bread for dipping.

Dutch Farmhouse Fondue

Serves 4–6

A soft and gentle fondue, mild enough for children.

1 garlic clove, crushed
15 ml/1 tbsp butter
450 g/1 lb/4 cups Gouda cheese, grated
15 ml/1 tbsp cornflour (cornstarch)
20 ml/4 tsp mustard powder
A pinch of grated nutmeg
300 ml/½ pt/1¼ cup full-cream milk
Salt and freshly ground black pepper
Cubed bread, to serve

Place all the ingredients in a deep 2.5 litre/4½ pt/11 cup glass or pottery dish, seasoning well to taste. Cook, uncovered, on Full for 7–9 minutes, stirring four times, until the fondue begins to bubble gently. Bring the dish to the table and eat by spearing a cube of bread on to a long fondue fork, swirling it round in the cheese mixture, then lifting it out.

Farmhouse Fondue with a Kick

Serves 4–6

Prepare as for Dutch Farmhouse Fondue, but stir in 30–45 ml/2–3 tbsp Genever (Dutch gin) after cooking.

Baked Egg Flamenco Style

Serves 1

Melted butter or margarine

1 small tomato, blanched, skinned and chopped

2 spring onions (scallions), chopped

1–2 stuffed olives, sliced

5 ml/1 tsp oil

15 ml/1 tbsp cooked ham, finely chopped

1 egg

Salt and freshly ground black pepper

15 ml/1 tbsp double (heavy) cream or crème fraîche

5 ml/1 tsp very finely chopped parsley, chives or coriander (cilantro)

Brush a small ramekin dish (custard cup) or individual soufflé dish with melted butter or margarine. Add the tomato, spring onions, olives, oil and ham. Cover with a saucer and heat through on Full for 1 minute. Gently break in the egg and puncture the yolk twice with a skewer or the tip of a knife. Season well to taste. Coat with the cream and sprinkle with the herbs. Cover as before and cook on Defrost for 3 minutes. Allow to stand for 1 minute before eating.

Bread and Butter Cheese and Parsley Pudding

Serves 4–6

4 large slices white bread

50 g/2 oz/¼ cup butter, at kitchen temperature

175 g/6 oz/1½ cups orange-coloured Cheddar cheese

45 ml/3 tbsp chopped parsley

600 ml/1 pt/2½ cups cold milk

3 eggs

5 ml/1 tsp salt

Paprika

Spread the bread with the butter and cut each slice into four squares. Thoroughly butter a 1.75 litre/3 pt/7½ cup dish. Arrange half the bread squares, buttered sides up, over the base of the dish. Sprinkle with two-thirds of the cheese and all the parsley. Arrange the remaining bread on top, buttered sides up. Pour the milk into a jug and warm, uncovered, on Full for 3 minutes. Beat the eggs until foamy, then gradually whisk in the milk. Stir in the salt. Pour gently over the bread and butter. Sprinkle the remaining cheese on top and dust with paprika. Cover with kitchen paper and cook on Defrost for 30 minutes. Allow to stand for 5 minutes, then brown under a hot grill (broiler), if liked, before serving.

Bread and Butter Cheese and Parsley Pudding with Cashew Nuts

Serves 4–6

Prepare as for Bread and Butter Cheese and Parsley Pudding, but add 45 ml/3 tbsp cashew nuts, toasted and coarsely chopped, with the cheese and parsley.

Four-cheese Bread and Butter Pudding

Serves 4–6

Prepare as for Bread and Butter Cheese and Parsley Pudding, but use a mixture of grated Cheddar, Edam, Red Leicester and crumbled Stilton cheeses. Substitute four chopped pickled onions for the parsley.

Cheese and Egg Crumpets

Serves 4

300 ml/10 fl oz/1 can condensed mushroom soup
45 ml/3 tbsp single (light) cream
125 g/4 oz/1 cup Red Leicester cheese, grated
4 hot toasted crumpets
4 freshly poached eggs

Put the soup, cream and half the cheese into a 900 ml/1½ pt/3¾ cup bowl. Heat, uncovered, on Full for 4–5 minutes until hot and smooth, beating every minute. Put each crumpet on a warmed plate and top with an egg. Coat with the mushroom mixture, sprinkle with the remaining cheese and heat one at a time on Full for about 1 minute until the cheese is melted and bubbling. Eat straight away.

Upside-down Cheese and Tomato Pudding

Serves 4

225 g/8 oz/2 cups self-raising (self-rising) flour

5 ml/1 tsp mustard powder

5 ml/1 tsp salt

125 g/4 oz/½ cup butter or margarine

125 g/4 oz/1 cup Edam or Cheddar cheese, grated

2 eggs, beaten

150 ml/¼ pt/2/3 cup cold milk

4 large tomatoes, blanched and skinned and chopped

15 ml/1 tbsp chopped parsley or coriander (cilantro)

Grease a deep round 1.75 litre/3 pt/7½ cup pudding basin with butter. Sift the flour, mustard powder and 2.5 ml/½ tsp of the salt into a bowl. Rub in the butter or margarine finely, then toss in the cheese. Mix to a soft consistency with the eggs and milk. Spread smoothly into the prepared basin. Cook, uncovered, on Full for 6 minutes. Mix the tomatoes with the remaining salt. Place in a shallow bowl and cover with a plate. Remove the pudding from the oven and carefully invert into a shallow dish. Cover with kitchen paper and cook on Full for a further 2 minutes. Remove from the oven and cover with a piece of foil to retain the heat. Put the tomatoes in the microwave and heat on Full for 3 minutes. Spoon over the pudding, sprinkle with the herbs and serve hot.

Pizza Crumpets

Serves 4

45 ml/3 tbsp tomato purée (paste)

30 ml/2 tbsp olive oil

1 garlic clove, crushed

4 hot toasted crumpets

2 tomatoes, thinly sliced

175 g/6 oz Mozzarella cheese, sliced

12 black olives

Mix together the tomato purée, olive oil and garlic and spread on to the crumpets. Arrange the tomato slices on top. Cover with the cheese and stud with the olives. Heat one at a time on Full for about 1–1½ minutes until the cheese is starting to melt. Eat straight away.

Gingered Sea Bass with Onions

Serves 8

A Cantonese speciality and a typical Chinese buffet dish.

2 sea bass, 450 g/1 lb each, cleaned but heads left on
8 spring onions (scallions)
5 ml/1 tsp salt
2.5 ml/½ tsp sugar
2.5 cm/1 in piece fresh root ginger, peeled and finely chopped
45 ml/3 tbsp soy sauce

Wash the fish inside and out. Dry with kitchen paper. Make three diagonal slashes with a sharp knife, about 2.5 cm/1 in apart, on both sides of each fish. Place head-to-tail in a 30 3 20 cm/12 3 8 in dish. Top and tail the onions, cut each into threads along its length and sprinkle over the fish. Thoroughly mix together the remaining ingredients and use to coat the fish. Cover the dish with clingfilm (plastic wrap) and slit it twice to allow steam to escape. Cook on Full for 12 minutes, turning the dish once. Transfer the fish to a serving plate and coat with the onions and juices from dish.

Trout Packets

Serves 2

Professional chefs call this truites en papillote. The parcels of simply prepared delicate trout make a smart fish course.

2 large cleaned trout, 450 g/1 lb each, washed but heads left on
1 onion, thickly sliced
1 small lemon or lime, thickly sliced
2 large dried bay leaves, coarsely crumbled
2.5 ml/½ tsp herbes de Provence
5 ml/1 tsp salt

Prepare two rectangles of baking parchment, 40 3 35 cm/16 3 14 in each. Place the onion and lemon or lime slices in the cavities of the fish with the bay leaves. Transfer to the parchment rectangles and sprinkle with the herbs and salt. Wrap each trout individually, then put both parcels together in a shallow dish. Cook on Full for 14 minutes, turning the dish once. Allow to stand for 2 minutes. Transfer each to a warmed plate and open out the parcels at the table.

Shining Monkfish with Slender Beans

Serves 4

125 g/4 oz French (green) or Kenya beans, topped and tailed
150 ml/¼ pt/2/3 cup boiling water
450 g/1 lb monkfish
15 ml/1 tbsp cornflour (cornstarch)
1.5–2.5 ml/¼–½ tsp Chinese five spice powder
45 ml/3 tbsp rice wine or medium sherry
5 ml/1 tsp bottled oyster sauce
2.5 ml/½ tsp sesame oil
1 garlic clove, crushed
50 ml/2 fl oz/3½ tbsp hot water
15 ml/1 tbsp soy sauce
Egg noodles, to serve

Halve the beans. Place in a round 1.25 litre/2¼ pt/5½ cup dish. Add the boiling water. Cover with clingfilm (plastic wrap) and slit it twice to allow steam to escape. Cook on Full for 4 minutes. Drain and set aside. Wash the monkfish and cut it into narrow strips. Mix the cornflour and spice powder with the rice wine or sherry until smooth. Stir in the remaining ingredients. Transfer to the dish in which the beans were cooked. Cook, uncovered, on Full for 1½ minutes. Stir until smooth, then mix in the beans and monkfish. Cover as before and cook on Full for 4 minutes. Allow to stand for 2 minutes, then stir round and serve.

Shining Prawns with Mangetout

Serves 4

Prepare as for Shining Monkfish with Slender Beans, but substitute mangetout (snow peas) for the beans and cook them for only 2½–3 minutes as they should remain crisp. Substitute shelled prawns (shrimp) for the monkfish.

Normandy Cod with Cider and Calvados

Serves 4

50 g/2 oz/¼ cup butter or margarine

1 onion, very thinly sliced

3 carrots, very thinly sliced

50 g/2 oz mushrooms, trimmed and thinly sliced

4 large cod steaks, about 225 g/8 oz each

5 ml/1 tsp salt

150 ml/¼ pt/2/3 cup cider

15 ml/1 tbsp cornflour (cornstarch)

25 ml/1½ tbsp cold water

15 ml/1 tbsp calvados

Parsley, to garnish

Place half the butter or margarine in a deep 20 cm/8 in diameter dish. Melt, uncovered, on Full for 45–60 seconds. Mix in the onion, carrots and mushrooms. Arrange the fish in a single layer on top. Dust with the salt. Pour the cider into the dish and dot the steaks with the remaining butter or margarine. Cover with clingfilm (plastic wrap) and slit it twice to allow steam to escape. Cook on Full for 8 minutes, turning the dish four times. Carefully pour off the cooking liquor and reserve. Mix the cornflour smoothly with the water and calvados. Add the fish juices. Cook, uncovered, on Full for 2–2½ minutes until the sauce thickens, whisking every 30 seconds. Arrange the fish on a warmed serving plate and top with the vegetables. Coat with the sauce and garnish with parsley.

Fish Paella

Serves 6–8

Spain's foremost rice dish, known worldwide through international travel.

900 g/2 lb skinned salmon fillet, cubed
1 packet saffron powder
60 ml/4 tbsp hot water
30 ml/2 tbsp olive oil
2 onions, chopped
2 garlic cloves, crushed
1 green (bell) pepper, seeded and coarsely chopped
225 g/8 oz/1 cup Italian or Spanish risotto rice
175 g/6 oz/1½ cups frozen or fresh peas
600 ml/1 pt/2½ cups boiling water
7.5 ml/1½ tsp salt
3 tomatoes, blanched, peeled and quartered
75 g/3 oz/¾ cup cooked ham, diced
125 g/4 oz/1 cup peeled prawns (shrimp)
250 g/9 oz/1 large can mussels in brine
Lemon wedges or slices, to garnish

Arrange the salmon cubes round the edge of a 25 cm/10 in diameter casserole dish (Dutch oven), leaving a small hollow in the centre. Cover the dish with clingfilm (plastic wrap) and slit it twice to allow steam to escape. Cook on Defrost for 10–11 minutes, turning the dish twice, until the fish looks flaky and just cooked. Drain off and reserve the liquid and set aside the salmon. Wash and dry the dish. Empty the saffron into a small bowl, add the hot water and leave to soak for 10 minutes. Pour the oil into the cleaned dish and add the onions, garlic and green pepper. Cook, uncovered, on Full for 4 minutes. Add the rice, saffron and soaking water, peas, salmon cubes, reserved salmon liquid, boiling water and salt. Mix thoroughly but gently. Cover as before and cook on Full for 10 minutes. Allow to stand in the microwave for 10 minutes. Cook on Full for a further 5 minutes. Uncover and carefully mix in the tomatoes and ham. Garnish with the prawns, mussels and lemon and serve.

Soused Herrings

Serves 4

4 herring, about 450 g/1 lb each, filleted

2 large bay leaves, coarsely crumbled

15 ml/1 tbsp mixed pickling spice

2 onions, sliced and separated into rings

150 ml/¼ pt/2/3 cup boiling water

20 ml/4 tsp granulated sugar

10 ml/2 tsp salt

90 ml/6 tbsp malt vinegar

Buttered bread, to serve

Roll up each herring fillet from the head to the tail end, skin sides inside. Arrange round the edge of a deep 25 cm/10 in diameter dish. Sprinkle with the bay leaves and spice. Arrange the onion rings between the herrings. Thoroughly mix together the remaining ingredients and spoon over the fish. Cover with clingfilm (plastic wrap) and slit it twice to allow steam to escape. Cook on Full for 18 minutes. Allow to cool, then chill. Eat cold with bread and butter.

Moules Marinières

Serves 4

Belgium's national dish, always served with a side dish of chips (fries).

900 ml/2 pts/5 cups fresh mussels

15 g/½ oz/1 tbsp butter or margarine

1 small onion, chopped

1 garlic clove, crushed

150 ml/¼ pt/2/3 cup dry white wine

1 bouquet garni sachet

1 dried bay leaf, crumbled

7.5 ml/1½ tsp salt

20 ml/4 tsp fresh white breadcrumbs

20 ml/4 tsp chopped parsley

Wash the mussels under cold running water. Scrape away any barnacles, then cut off the beards. Discard any mussels with cracked shells or those that are open; they can cause food poisoning. Wash again. Put the butter or margarine in a deep bowl. Melt, uncovered, on Full for about 30 seconds. Mix in the onion and garlic. Cover with a plate and cook on Full for 6 minutes, stirring twice. Add the wine, bouquet garni, bay leaf, salt and mussels. Stir gently to mix. Cover as before and cook on Full for 5 minutes. Using a slotted spoon, transfer the mussels into four deep bowls or soup plates. Stir the breadcrumbs and half the parsley into the cooking liquid, then spoon over the mussels. Sprinkle with the remaining parsley and serve straight away.

Mackerel with Rhubarb and Raisin Sauce

The prettily coloured sweet-sour sauce balances the rich mackerel beautifully.

350 g/12 oz young rhubarb, coarsely chopped

60 ml/4 tbsp boiling water

30 ml/2 tbsp raisins

30 ml/2 tbsp granulated sugar

2.5 ml/½ tsp vanilla essence (extract)

Finely grated zest and juice of ½ small lemon

4 mackerel, cleaned, boned and heads discarded

50 g/2 oz/¼ cup butter or margarine

Salt and freshly ground black pepper

Place the rhubarb and water in a casserole dish (Dutch oven). Cover with clingfilm (plastic wrap) and slit it twice to allow steam to escape. Cook on Full for 6 minutes, turning the dish three times. Uncover and mash the rhubarb to a pulp. Stir in the raisins, sugar, vanilla essence and lemon zest, then set aside. With the skin sides facing you, fold each mackerel in half crossways from head to tail. Put the butter or margarine and lemon juice in a deep 20 cm/8 in diameter dish. Melt on Full for 2 minutes. Add the fish and coat with the melted ingredients. Sprinkle with salt and pepper. Cover with clingfilm (plastic wrap) and slit it twice to allow steam to escape. Cook on Medium for 14–16 minutes until the fish looks flaky. Allow to stand for 2 minutes. Heat through the rhubarb sauce on Full for 1 minute and serve with the mackerel.

Herring with Apple Cider Sauce

Serves 4

Prepare as for Mackerel with Rhubarb and Raisin Sauce, but substitute peeled and cored cooking (tart) apples for the rhubarb and boiling cider in place of the water. Omit the raisins.

Carp in Jellied Sauce

Serves 4

1 very fresh carp, cleaned and cut into 8 thin slices
30 ml/2 tbsp malt vinegar
3 carrots, thinly sliced
3 onions, thinly sliced
600 ml/1 pt/2½ cups boiling water
10–15 ml/2–3 tsp salt

Wash the carp, then soak for 3 hours in enough cold water with the vinegar added to cover the fish. (This removes the muddy taste.) Place the carrots and onions in a deep 23 cm/9 in diameter dish with the boiling water and salt. Cover with clingfilm (plastic wrap) and slit it twice to allow steam to escape. Cook on Full for 20 minutes, turning the dish four times. Drain, reserving the liquid. (The vegetables can be used elsewhere in fish soup or stir-fries.) Pour the liquid back into the dish. Add the carp in a single layer. Cover as before and cook on Full for 8 minutes, turning the dish twice. Allow to stand for 3 minutes. Using a fish slice, transfer the carp to a shallow dish. Cover and chill. Transfer the liquid into a jug and chill until lightly jellied. Spoon the jelly over the fish and serve.

Rollmops with Apricots

Serves 4

75 g/3 oz dried apricots
150 ml/¼ pt/2/3 cup cold water
3 bought rollmops with sliced onions
150 g/5 oz/2/3 cup crème fraîche
Mixed salad leaves
Crispbread

Wash the apricots and cut into bite-sized pieces. Place in a bowl with the cold water. Cover with an inverted plate and heat on Full for 5 minutes. Allow to stand for 5 minutes. Drain. Cut the rollmops into strips. Add to the apricots with the onions and crème fraîche. Mix well. Cover and leave to marinate in the refrigerator for 4–5 hours. Serve on salad leaves with crispbread.

Poached Kipper

Serves 1

*Microwaving stops the smell permeating the house and leaves the
kipper juicy and tender.*

1 large undyed kipper, about 450 g/1 lb
120 ml/4 fl oz/½ cup cold water
Butter or margarine

Trim the kipper, discarding the tail. Soak for 3–4 hours in several
changes of cold water to reduce saltiness, if wished, then drain. Place
in a large, shallow dish with the water. Cover with clingfilm (plastic
wrap) and slit it twice to allow steam to escape. Cook on Full for 4
minutes. Serve on a warmed plate with knob of butter or margarine.

Prawns Madras

Serves 4

25 g/1 oz/2 tbsp ghee or 15 ml/1 tbsp groundnut (peanut) oil

2 onions, chopped

2 garlic cloves, crushed

15 ml/1 tbsp hot curry powder

5 ml/1 tsp ground cumin

5 ml/1 tsp garam masala

Juice of 1 small lime

150 ml/¼ pt/2/3 cup fish or vegetable stock

30 ml/2 tbsp tomato purée (paste)

60 ml/4 tbsp sultanas (golden raisins)

450 g/1 lb/4 cups peeled prawns (shrimp), thawed if frozen

175 g/6 oz/¾ cup long-grain rice, boiled

Popadoms

Put the ghee or oil in a deep 20 cm/8 in diameter dish. Heat, uncovered, on Full for 1 minute. Thoroughly mix in the onions and garlic. Cook, uncovered, on Full for 3 minutes. Add the curry powder, cumin, garam masala and lime juice. Cook, uncovered, on Full for 3 minutes, stirring twice. Add the stock, tomato purée and sultanas. Cover with an inverted plate and cook on Full for 5 minutes. Drain the prawns if necessary, then add to the dish and stir round to combine. Cook, uncovered, on Full for 1½ minutes. Serve with the rice and popadoms.

Martini Plaice Rolls with Sauce

Serves 4

8 plaice fillets, 175 g/6 oz each, washed and dried

Salt and freshly ground black pepper

Juice of 1 lemon

2.5 ml/½ tsp Worcestershire sauce

25 g/1 oz/2 tbsp butter or margarine

4 shallots, peeled and chopped

100 g/3½ oz/1 cup cooked ham, cut into strips

400 g/14 oz mushrooms, thinly sliced

20 ml/4 tsp cornflour (cornstarch)

20 ml/4 tsp cold milk

250 ml/8 fl oz/1 cup chicken stock

150 g/¼ pt/2/3 cup single (light) cream

2.5 ml/½ tsp caster (superfine) sugar

1.5 ml/¼ tsp turmeric

10 ml/2 tsp martini bianco

Season the fish with salt and pepper. Marinate in the lemon juice and Worcestershire sauce for 15–20 minutes. Melt the butter or margarine in a saucepan (skillet). Add the shallots and fry (sauté) gently until soft and semi-transparent. Add the ham and mushrooms and stir-fry for 7 minutes. Blend the cornflour with the cold milk until smooth and add the remaining ingredients. Roll up the plaice fillets and spear with cocktail sticks (toothpicks). Arrange in a deep 20 cm/8 in diameter dish. Coat with the mushroom mixture. Cover with clingfilm (plastic wrap) and slit it twice to allow steam to escape. Cook on Full for 10 minutes.

Shellfish Ragout with Walnuts

Serves 4

30 ml/2 tbsp olive oil

1 onion, peeled and chopped

2 carrots, peeled and finely diced

3 celery stalks, cut into narrow strips

1 red (bell) pepper, seeded and cut into strips

1 green (bell) pepper, seeded and cut into strips

1 small courgette (zucchini), trimmed and thinly sliced

250 ml/8 fl oz/1 cup rosé wine

1 bouquet garni sachet

325 ml/11 fl oz/11/3 cups vegetable or fish stock

400 g/14 oz/1 large can chopped tomatoes

125 g/4 oz squid rings

125 g/4 oz cooked shelled mussels

200 g/7 oz lemon sole or flounder fillet, cut into chunks

4 giant prawns (jumbo shrimp), cooked

50 g/2 oz/½ cup walnuts, coarsely chopped

30 ml/2 tbsp stoned (pitted) black olives

10 ml/2 tsp gin

Juice of ½ small lemon

2.5 ml/½ tsp granulated sugar

1 baguette

30 ml/2 tbsp coarsely chopped basil leaves

Pour the oil into a 2.5 litre/4½ pt/11 cup dish. Heat, uncovered, on Full for 2 minutes. Add the prepared vegetables and toss in the oil to coat. Cover with clingfilm (plastic wrap) and slit it twice to allow steam to escape. Cook on Full for 5 minutes. Add the wine and bouquet garni. Cover as before and cook on Full for 5 minutes. Add the stock, tomatoes and fish. Re-cover and cook on Full for 10 minutes. Mix in all the remaining ingredients except the basil. Re-cover and cook on full for 4 minutes. Scatter with the basil and serve hot.

Cod Hot-pot

Serves 4

25 g/1 oz/2 tbsp butter or margarine

1 onion, peeled and chopped

2 carrots, peeled and finely diced

2 celery stalks, thinly sliced

150 ml/¼ pt/2/3 cup medium-dry white wine

400 g/14 oz skinned cod fillet, cut into large cubes

15 ml/1 tbsp cornflour (cornstarch)

75 ml/5 tbsp cold milk

350 ml/12 fl oz/1½ cups fish or vegetable stock

Salt and freshly ground black pepper

75 ml/5 tbsp chopped dill (dill weed)

300 ml/½ pt/1¼ cups double (heavy) cream, softly whipped

2 egg yolks

Place the butter or margarine in a 20 cm/8 in diameter casserole dish (Dutch oven). Heat, uncovered, on Full for 2 minutes. Mix in the vegetables and wine. Cover with clingfilm (plastic wrap) and slit it twice to allow steam to escape. Cook on Full for 5 minutes. Allow to stand for 3 minutes. Uncover. Add the fish to the vegetables. Mix the cornflour with the cold milk until smooth, then add to the casserole with the stock. Season. Cover as before and cook on Full for 8 minutes. Add the dill. Thoroughly mix the cream with the egg yolks and stir into the casserole. Cover and cook on Full for 1½ minutes.

Smoked Cod Hot-pot

Serves 4

Prepare as for Cod Hot-pot but substitute smoked cod fillet for fresh.

Monkfish in Golden Lemon Cream Sauce

Serves 6

300 ml/½ pt/1¼ cups full-cream milk

25 g/1 oz/2 tbsp butter or margarine, at kitchen temperature

675 g/1½ lb monkfish fillets, cut into bite-sized chunks

45 ml/3 tbsp plain (all-purpose) flour

2 large egg yolks

Juice of 1 large lemon

2.5–5 ml/½ –1 tsp salt

2.5 ml/½ tsp finely chopped tarragon

Cooked vol-au-vent cases (patty shells) or toasted ciabatta bread slices

Pour the milk into a jug and warm, uncovered, on Full for 2 minutes. Place the butter or margarine in a deep 20 cm/8 in diameter dish. Melt, uncovered, on Defrost for 1½ minutes. Coat the fish chunks in flour and add to the butter or margarine in the dish. Gently pour in the milk. Cover with clingfilm (plastic wrap) and slit it twice to allow steam to escape. Cook on Full for 7 minutes. Beat together the egg yolks, lemon juice and salt and stir into the fish. Cook, uncovered, on Full for 2 minutes. Allow to stand for 5 minutes. Stir round, sprinkle with the tarragon and serve in vol-au-vent cases or with slices of toasted ciabatta.

Sole in Golden Lemon Cream Sauce

Serves 6

Prepare as for Monkfish in Golden Lemon Cream Sauce, but substitute sole, cut into strips, for the monkfish chunks.

Salmon Hollandaise

Serves 4

4 salmon steaks, 175–200 g/6–7 oz each
150 ml/¼ pt water/2/3 cup water or dry white wine
2.5 ml/½ tsp salt
Hollandaise Sauce

Arrange the steaks round the sides of a deep 20 cm/8 in diameter dish. Add the water or wine. Sprinkle the fish with the salt. Cover with clingfilm (plastic wrap) and slit it twice to allow steam to escape. Cook on Defrost (to prevent the salmon spitting) for 16–18 minutes. Allow to stand for 4 minutes. Lift out on to four warmed plates with a fish slice, draining off the liquid. Coat each with the Hollandaise Sauce.

Serves 4

Prepare as for Salmon Hollandaise, but add 30 ml/2 tbsp chopped coriander (cilantro) to the sauce as soon as it has finished cooking. For additional flavour, mix in 10 ml/2 tsp chopped lemon balm.

Salmon Mayonnaise Flake

Serves 6

900 g/2 lb fresh salmon fillet, skinned

Salt and freshly ground black pepper

Melted butter or margarine (optional)

50 g/2 oz/½ cup flaked (slivered) almonds, toasted

1 small onion, finely chopped

30 ml/2 tbsp finely chopped parsley

5 ml/1 tsp chopped tarragon

200 ml/7 fl oz/scant 1 cup French-style mayonnaise

Lettuce leaves

Fennel sprays, to garnish

Divide the salmon into four portions. Arrange round the edge of a deep 25 cm/10 in diameter dish. Sprinkle with salt and pepper and trickle a little melted butter or margarine over the top if wished. Cover with clingfilm (plastic wrap) and slit it twice to allow steam to escape. Cook on Defrost for 20 minutes. Allow to cool to lukewarm, then flake the fish with two forks. Transfer to a bowl, add half the almonds and the onion, parsley and tarragon. Gently stir in the mayonnaise until well mixed and moist. Line a long serving dish with lettuce leaves. Arrange a line of salmon mayonnaise on top. Sprinkle with the remaining almonds and garnish with fennel.

Mediterranean-style Salmon Roast

Serves 6–8

1.5 kg/3lb portion middle-cut salmon
60 ml/4 tbsp olive oil
60 ml/4 tbsp lemon juice
60 ml/4 tbsp tomato purée (paste)
15 ml/1 tbsp chopped basil leaves
7.5 ml/1½ tsp salt
45 ml/3 tbsp small capers, drained
45 ml/3 tbsp chopped parsley

Wash the salmon, ensuring all scales are scraped off. Place in a deep 20 cm/8 in diameter dish. Whisk together the remaining ingredients and spoon over the fish. Cover with a plate and leave to marinate in the refrigerator for 3 hours. Cover with clingfilm (plastic wrap) and slit it twice to allow steam to escape. Cook on Full for 20 minutes, turning the dish twice. Divide into portions to serve.

Kedgeree with Curry

Serves 4

Once a breakfast dish, particularly associated with colonial days in India around the turn of the century, kedgeree is now more often served for lunch.

350 g/12 oz smoked haddock or cod fillet
60 ml/4 tbsp cold water
50 g/2 oz/¼ cup butter or margarine
225 g/8 oz/1 cup basmati rice
15 ml/1 tbsp mild curry powder
600 ml/1 pt/2½ cups boiling water
3 hard-boiled (hard-cooked) eggs
150 ml/¼ pt/2/3 cup single (light) cream
15 ml/1 tbsp chopped parsley
Salt and freshly ground black pepper
Parsley sprigs, to garnish

Put the fish into a shallow dish with the cold water. Cover with clingfilm (plastic wrap) and slit it twice to allow steam to escape. Cook on Full for 5 minutes. Drain. Flake up the flesh with two forks, removing the skin and bones. Place the butter or margarine in a round 1.75 litre/3 pt/7½ cup heatproof serving dish and melt on Defrost for 1½–2 minutes. Stir in the rice, curry powder and boiling water. Cover as before and cook on Full for 15 minutes. Chop two of the eggs and stir into the dish with the fish, cream and parsley, seasoning to taste.

Fork round, cover with an inverted plate and reheat on Full for 5 minutes. Slice the remaining egg. Remove the dish from the microwave and garnish with the sliced egg and parsley sprigs.

Kedgeree with Smoked Salmon

Serves 4

Prepare as for Kedgeree with Curry, but substitute 225 g/8 oz smoked salmon (lox), cut into strips, for the smoked haddock or cod. Smoked salmon does not need precooking.

Serves 6

175 g/6 oz shortcrust pastry (basic pie crust)
1 egg yolk, beaten
125 g/4 oz smoked fish such as mackerel, haddock, cod or trout,
cooked and flaked
3 eggs
150 ml/¼ pt/2/3 cup soured (dairy sour) cream
30 ml/2 tbsp mayonnaise
Salt and freshly ground black pepper
75 g/3 oz/¾ cup Cheddar cheese, grated
Paprika
Mixed salad

Lightly butter a fluted 20 cm/8 in diameter glass or china flan dish.
Roll out the pastry and use to line the greased dish. Prick well all over,
especially where the side meets the base. Cook, uncovered, on Full for
6 minutes, turning the dish twice. If any bulges appear, press down
with fingers protected by oven gloves. Brush the inside of the pastry
case (pie shell) with the egg yolk. Cook on Full for 1 minute to seal
any holes. Remove from the oven. Cover the base with the fish. Beat
the eggs with the cream and mayonnaise, seasoning to taste. Pour into
the quiche and sprinkle with the cheese and paprika. Cook, uncovered,
on Full for 8 minutes. Serve warm with salad.

Louisiana Prawn Gumbo

Serves 8

3 onions, chopped

2 garlic cloves

3 celery stalks, finely chopped

1 green (bell) pepper, seeded and finely chopped

50 g/2 oz/¼ cup butter

60 ml/4 tbsp plain (all-purpose) flour

900 ml/1½ pt/3¾ cups hot vegetable or chicken stock

350 g/12 oz okra (ladies' fingers), topped and tailed

15 ml/1 tbsp salt

10 ml/2 tsp ground coriander (cilantro)

5 ml/1 tsp turmeric

2.5 ml/½ tsp ground allspice

30 ml/2 tbsp lemon juice

2 bay leaves

5–10 ml/1–2 tsp Tabasco sauce

450 g/1 lb/4 cups cooked peeled prawns (shrimp), thawed if frozen

350 g/12 oz/1½ cups long-grain rice, boiled

Place the onions in a 2.5 litre/4½ pt/11 cup bowl. Crush the garlic over the top. Add the celery and green pepper. Melt the butter on Full for 2 minutes. Stir in the flour. Cook, uncovered, on Full for 5–7 minutes, stirring four times and watching carefully in case of burning, until the mixture is a light biscuit-coloured roux. Gradually blend in the stock.

Set aside. Cut the okra into chunks and add to the vegetables with all the remaining ingredients except the Tabasco and prawns but including the roux mix. Cover with clingfilm (plastic wrap) and slit it twice to allow steam to escape. Cook on Full for 25 minutes. Allow to stand for 5 minutes. Stir in the Tabasco and prawns. Spoon into warmed deep bowls and add a mound of freshly cooked rice to each. Eat straight away.

Monkfish Gumbo

Serves 8

Prepare as for Louisiana Prawn Gumbo, but substitute the same weight of boned monkfish, cut into strips, for the prawns (shrimp). Cover with clingfilm (plastic wrap) and cook on Full for 4 minutes before transferring to serving bowls.

Mixed Fish Gumbo

Serves 8

Prepare as for Louisiana Prawn Gumbo, but substitute assorted cubed fish fillets for the prawns (shrimp).

Trout with Almonds

Serves 4

50 g/2 oz/¼ cup butter
15 ml/1 tbsp lemon juice
4 medium trout
50 g/2 oz/½ cup flaked (slivered) almonds, toasted
Salt and freshly ground black pepper
4 lemon wedges
Parsley sprigs

Melt the butter on Defrost for 1½ minutes. Stir in the lemon juice. Place the trout, head-to-tail, in a buttered 25 3 20 cm/10 3 8 in dish. Coat the fish with the butter mixture and sprinkle with the almonds and seasoning. Cover with clingfilm (plastic wrap) and slit it twice to allow steam to escape. Cook on Full for 9–12 minutes, turning the dish twice. Allow to stand for 5 minutes. Transfer to four warmed plates. Pour over the cooking liquid and garnish with the lemon wedges and parsley sprigs.

Prawns Provençale

Serves 4

225 g/8 oz/1 cup easy-cook long-grain rice
600 ml/1 pt/2½ cups hot fish or chicken stock
5 ml/1 tsp salt
15 ml/1 tbsp olive oil
1 onion, grated
1–2 garlic cloves, crushed
6 large very ripe tomatoes, blanched, skinned and chopped
15 ml/1 tbsp chopped basil leaves
5 ml/1 tsp dark soft brown sugar
450 g/1 lb/4 cups frozen peeled prawns (shrimp), unthawed
Salt and freshly ground black pepper
Chopped parsley

Place the rice in a 2 litre/3½ pt/8½ cup dish. Stir in the hot stock and salt. Cover with clingfilm (plastic wrap) and slit it twice to allow steam to escape. Cook on Full for 16 minutes. Allow to stand for 8 minutes for the rice to absorb all the moisture. Pour the oil into a 1.75 litre/3 pt/7½ cup serving dish. Heat, uncovered, on Full for 1½ minutes. Stir in the onion and garlic. Cook, uncovered, on Full for 3 minutes, stirring twice. Add the tomatoes with the basil and sugar. Cover with a plate and cook on Full for 5 minutes, stirring twice. Mix in the frozen prawns and seasoning to taste. Cover as before and cook on Full for 4 minutes, then gently separate the prawns. Re-cover and cook on Full for a further 3 minutes. Allow to stand. Cover the rice with a plate and reheat on Defrost for 5–6 minutes. Spoon on to four warmed plates and top with the fish and tomato mixture. Sprinkle with parsley and serve hot.

Plaice in Celery Sauce with Toasted Almonds

Serves 4

8 plaice fillets, total weight about 1 kg/2¼ lb
300 ml/10 fl oz/1 can condensed cream of celery soup
150 m/¼ pt/2/3 cup boiling water
15 ml/1 tbsp finely chopped parsley
30 ml/2 tbsp flaked (slivered) almonds, toasted

Roll up the fish fillets from head to tail, skin sides inside. Arrange round the edge of a deep 25 cm/10 in diameter buttered dish. Gently whisk together the soup and water and stir in the parsley. Spoon over the fish. Cover the dish with clingfilm (plastic wrap) and slit it twice to allow steam to escape. Cook on Full for 12 minutes, turning the dish twice. Allow to stand for 5 minutes. Cook on Full for a further 6 minutes. Spoon on to warmed plates and serve, sprinkled with the almonds.

Fillets in Tomato Sauce with Marjoram

Serves 4

Prepare as for Plaice in Celery Sauce with Toasted Almonds, but substitute condensed tomato soup for celery and 2.5 ml/½ tsp dried marjoram for the parsley.

Fillets in Mushroom Sauce with Watercress

Serves 4

Prepare as for Plaice in Celery Sauce with Toasted Almonds, but substitute condensed mushroom soup for celery and 30 ml/2 tbsp chopped watercress for the parsley.

Hashed Cod with Poached Eggs

Serves 4

This was found in a handwritten nineteenth-century notebook, belonging to the grandmother of an old friend.

675 g/1½ lb skinned cod fillet

10 ml/2 tsp melted butter or margarine or sunflower oil

Paprika

Salt and freshly ground black pepper

50 g/2 oz/¼ cup butter or margarine

8 large spring onions (scallions), trimmed and chopped

350 g/12 oz cold cooked potatoes, diced

150 ml/¼ pt/2/3 cup single (light) cream

5 ml/1 tsp salt

4 eggs

175 ml/6 fl oz/¾ cup hot water

5 ml/1 tsp vinegar

Arrange the fish in a shallow dish. Brush with some of the melted butter or margarine or oil. Season with paprika, salt and pepper. Cover with clingfilm (plastic wrap) and slit it twice to allow steam to escape. Cook on Defrost for 14–16 minutes. Flake up the fish with two forks, removing the bones. Put the remaining butter, margarine or oil into a 20 cm/8 in diameter casserole dish (Dutch oven). Heat, uncovered, on Defrost for 1½ –2 minutes. Mix in the onions. Cover with a plate and cook on Full for 5 minutes. Stir in the fish with the potatoes, cream and salt. Cover as before and reheat on Full for 5–7 minutes until very hot, stirring once or twice. Keep hot. To poach the eggs, gently break two into a small dish and add half the water and half the vinegar. Puncture the yolks with the tip of a knife. Cover with a plate and cook on Full for 2 minutes. Allow to stand for 1 minute. Repeat with the remaining eggs, hot water and vinegar. Spoon helpings of the hash on to four warmed plates and top each with an egg.

Haddock and Vegetables in Cider Sauce

Serves 4

50 g/2 oz/¼ cup butter or margarine
1 onion, thinly sliced and separated into rings
3 carrots, thinly sliced
50 g/2 oz button mushrooms, sliced
4 pieces filleted and skinned haddock or other white fish
5 ml/1 tsp salt
150 ml/¼ pt/2/3 cups medium-sweet cider
10 ml/2 tsp cornflour (cornstarch)
15 ml/1 tbsp cold water

Place half the butter or margarine in a deep 20 cm/8 in diameter dish. Melt, uncovered, on Defrost for about 1½ minutes. Add the onion, carrots and mushrooms. Arrange the fish on top. Sprinkle with the salt. Pour the cider gently over the fish. Dot with the remaining butter or margarine. Cover with clingfilm (plastic wrap) and slit it twice to allow steam to escape. Cook on Full for 8 minutes. In a glass jug, blend the cornflour smoothly with the cold water and gently strain in the fish liquor. Cook, uncovered, on Full for 2½ minutes until thickened, whisking every minute. Pour over the fish and vegetables. Spoon on to warmed plates and eat straight away.

Seaside Pie

Serves 4

For the topping:
700 g/1½ lb floury potatoes, unpeeled weight
75 ml/5 tbsp boiling water
15 ml/1 tbsp butter or margarine
75 ml/5 tbsp milk or single (light) cream
Salt and freshly ground pepper
Grated nutmeg

For the sauce:
300 ml/½ pt/1¼ cups cold milk
30 ml/2 tbsp butter or margarine
20 ml/4 tsp plain (all-purpose) flour
75 ml/5 tbsp Red Leicester or coloured Cheddar cheese, grated
5 ml/1 tsp wholegrain mustard
5 ml/1 tsp Worcestershire sauce

For the fish mixture:
450 g/1 lb skinned white fish fillet, at kitchen temperature
Melted butter or margarine
Paprika
60 ml/4 tbsp Red Leicester or coloured Cheddar cheese, grated

To make the topping, wash and peel the potatoes and cut into large cubes. Put in a 1.5 litre/2½ pt/6 cup dish with the boiling water. Cover with clingfilm (plastic wrap) and slit it twice to allow steam to escape. Cook on Full for 15 minutes, turning the dish twice. Allow to stand for 5 minutes. Drain and mash thoroughly with the butter or margarine and milk or cream, beating until fluffy. Season to taste with salt, pepper and nutmeg.

To make the sauce, heat the milk, uncovered, on Full for 1½ minutes. Set aside. Melt the butter or margarine, uncovered, on Defrost for 1– 1½ minutes. Stir in the flour. Cook, uncovered, on Full for 30 seconds. Gradually blend in the milk. Cook on Full for about 4 minutes, beating every minute to ensure smoothness, until the sauce is thickened. Stir in the cheese with the remaining sauce ingredients.

To make the fish mixture, arrange the fillets in a shallow dish and brush with melted butter or margarine. Season with paprika, salt and pepper. Cover with clingfilm (plastic wrap) and slit it twice to allow steam to escape. Cook on Full for 5–6 minutes. Flake up the fish with two forks, removing any bones. Transfer to a buttered 1.75 litre/3 pt/7½ cup dish. Mix in the sauce. Cover with the potatoes and sprinkle with the cheese and extra paprika. Reheat, uncovered, on Full for 6–7 minutes.

Serves 2

2 frozen smoked haddock portions, 175 g/6 oz each
Freshly ground black pepper
1 small courgette (zucchini), sliced
1 small onion, thinly sliced
2 tomatoes, blanched, skinned and chopped
½ red (bell) pepper, seeded and cut into strips
15 ml/1 tbsp snipped chives

Arrange the fish in a deep 18 cm/7 in diameter dish. Season with pepper. Cover with clingfilm (plastic wrap) and slit it twice to allow steam to escape. Cook on Full for 8 minutes. Spoon the juices over the fish, then allow to stand for 1 minute. Place the vegetables in another medium-sized casserole dish (Dutch oven). Cover with a plate and cook on Full for 5 minutes, stirring once. Spoon the vegetables over the fish. Cover as before and cook on Full for 2 minutes. Sprinkle with the chives and serve.

Coley Fillets with Leek and Lemon Marmalade

Serves 2

An off-beat arrangement from Edinburgh's Sea Fish Authority, which also donated the next three recipes.

15 ml/1 tbsp butter
1 garlic clove, peeled and crushed
1 leek, slit and thinly sliced
2 coley fillets, 175 g/6 oz each, skinned
Juice of ½ lemon
10 ml/2 tsp lemon marmalade
Salt and freshly ground black pepper

Place the butter, garlic and leek in a deep 18 cm/7 in diameter dish. Cover with clingfilm (plastic wrap) and slit it twice to allow steam to escape. Cook on Full for 2½ minutes. Uncover. Arrange the fillets on top and sprinkle with half the lemon juice. Cover as before and cook on Full for 7 minutes. Transfer the fish to two warmed plates and keep hot. Mix the remaining lemon juice, the marmalade and seasoning into the fish juices and leek. Cover with a plate and cook on Full for 1½ minutes. Spoon over the fish and serve.

Seafish in a Jacket

Serves 4

4 baking potatoes, unpeeled but well scrubbed
450 g/1 lb white fish fillet, skinned and cubed
45 ml/3 tbsp butter or margarine
3 spring onions (scallions), trimmed and chopped
30 ml/2 tbsp wholegrain mustard
1.5 ml/¼ tsp paprika, plus extra for dusting
30–45 ml/2–3 tbsp plain yoghurt
Salt

Stand the potatoes directly on the turntable, cover with kitchen paper and cook on Full for 16 minutes. Wrap in a clean tea towel (dish cloth) and set aside. Place the fish in an 18 cm/7 in diameter casserole dish (Dutch oven) with the butter or margarine, spring onions, mustard and paprika. Cover with a plate and cook on Full for 7 minutes, stirring twice. Allow to stand for 2 minutes. Mix in the yoghurt and salt to taste. Cut a cross on top of each potato and squeeze gently to open out. Fill with the fish mixture, dust with paprika and eat hot.

Swedish Cod with Melted Butter and Egg

Serves 4

300 ml/½ pt/1¼ cups cold water

3 whole cloves

5 juniper berries

1 bay leaf, crumbled

2.5 ml/½ tsp mixed pickling spice

1 onion, quartered

10 ml/2 tsp salt

4 middle-cut fresh cod steaks, 225 g/8 oz each

75 g/3 oz/2/3 cup butter

2 hard-boiled (hard-cooked) eggs (pages 98–9), shelled and chopped

Put the water, cloves, juniper berries, bay leaf, pickling spice, onion quarters and salt in a glass jug. Cover with clingfilm (plastic wrap) and slit it twice to allow steam to escape. Cook on Full for 15 minutes. Strain. Place the fish in a deep 25 cm/10 in diameter dish and pour in the strained liquid. Cover with clingfilm and slit it twice to allow steam to escape. Cook on Full for 10 minutes, turning the dish twice. Transfer the fish to a warmed dish, using a fish slice, and keep hot. Melt the butter, uncovered, on Defrost for 2 minutes. Pour over the fish. Sprinkle with the chopped eggs and serve.

Seafood Stroganoff

Serves 4

30 ml/2 tbsp butter or margarine
1 garlic clove, crushed
1 onion, sliced
125 g/4 oz button mushrooms
700 g/1½ lb white fish fillet, skinned and cubed
150 ml/¼ pt/2/3 cup soured (dairy sour) cream or crème fraîche
Salt and freshly ground black pepper
30 ml/2 tbsp chopped parsley

Place the butter or margarine in a 20 cm/8 in diameter casserole dish (Dutch oven). Melt, uncovered, on Defrost for 2 minutes. Add the garlic, onion and mushrooms. Cover with clingfilm (plastic wrap) and slit it twice to allow steam to escape. Cook on Full for 3 minutes. Add the fish cubes. Cover as before and cook on Full for 8 minutes. Stir in the cream and season with salt and pepper. Cover again and cook on Full for 1½ minutes. Serve sprinkled with the parsley.

Fresh Tuna Stroganoff

Serves 4

Prepare as for Seafood Stroganoff, but substitute very fresh tuna for the white fish.

White Fish Ragout Supreme

Serves 4

30 ml/2 tbsp butter or margarine

1 onion, chopped

2 carrots, finely diced

6 celery stalks, thinly sliced

150 ml/¼ pt/2/3 cup white wine

400 g/14 oz skinned cod or haddock fillet, cubed

10 ml/2 tsp cornflour (cornstarch)

90 ml/6 tbsp single (light) cream

150 ml/¼ pt/2/3 cup vegetable stock

Salt and freshly ground black pepper

2.5 ml/½ tsp anchovy essence (extract) or Worcestershire sauce

30 ml/2 tbsp chopped dill (dill weed)

300 ml/½ pt/1¼ cups whipping cream

2 egg yolks

Place the butter or margarine in a 20 cm/8 in diameter casserole dish (Dutch oven). Heat, uncovered, on Full for 2 minutes. Add the vegetables and wine. Cover with clingfilm (plastic wrap) and slit it twice to allow steam to escape. Cook on Full for 5 minutes. Allow to stand for 3 minutes. Add the fish to the vegetables. Blend the cornflour smoothly with the cream, then mix in the stock. Season with salt, pepper and the anchovy essence or Worcestershire sauce. Pour over the fish. Cover as before and cook on Full for 8 minutes. Mix in the dill, then beat together the cream and egg yolks and stir into the fish mixture. Cover as before and cook on Defrost for 3 minutes.

Salmon Mousse

Serves 8

30 ml/2 tbsp powdered gelatine

150 ml/¼ pt/2/3 cup cold water

418 g/15 oz/1 large can red salmon

150 ml/¼ pt/2/3 cup creamy mayonnaise

15 ml/1 tbsp mild made mustard

10 ml/2 tsp Worcestershire sauce

30 ml/2 tbsp fruit chutney, chopped if necessary

Juice of ½ large lemon

2 large egg whites

A pinch of salt

Cress, cucumber slices, salad greens and slices of fresh lime, to garnish

Stir the gelatine into 75 ml/5 tbsp of the cold water and allow to stand for 5 minutes to soften. Melt, uncovered, on Defrost for 2½–3 minutes. Stir again and mix in the remaining water. Tip the contents of the can of salmon into a fairly large bowl and flake with a fork, removing any skin and bones, then mash fairly finely. Mix in the melted gelatine, the mayonnaise, mustard, Worcestershire sauce, chutney and lemon juice. Cover and chill until just beginning to thicken and set round the edges. Beat the egg whites to stiff peaks. Beat one-third into the setting salmon mixture with the salt. Fold in the remaining egg whites and transfer the mixture to a 1.5 litre/2½ pt/6 cup ring mould, first rinsed with cold water. Cover with clingfilm (plastic wrap) and chill for 8 hours until firm. Before serving, quickly dip the mould up to its rim in and out of cold water to loosen. Run a wet knife gently round the sides, then invert on to a large wetted serving dish. (The wetting stops the jelly sticking.) Garnish attractively with plenty of cress, cucumber slices, salad greens and lime slices.

Dieters' Salmon Mousse

Serves 8

Prepare as for Salmon Mousse, but substitute fromage frais or quark for the mayonnaise.

Crab Mornay

Serves 4

300 ml/½ pt/1¼ cups full-cream milk

10 ml/2 tsp mixed pickling spice

1 small onion, cut into 8 wedges

2 parsley sprigs

A pinch of nutmeg

30 ml/2 tbsp butter

30 ml/2 tbsp plain (all-purpose) flour

Salt and freshly ground black pepper

75 g/3 oz/¾ cup Gruyère (Swiss) cheese, grated

5 ml/1 tsp continental mustard

350 g/12 oz prepared light and dark crabmeat

Toast slices

Pour the milk into a glass or plastic jug and stir in the pickling spice, onion wedges, parsley and nutmeg. Cover with a plate and heat on Full for 5–6 minutes until the milk just begins to shiver. Strain. Put the butter into a 1.5 litre/2½ pt/6 cup bowl and melt on Defrost for 1½ minutes. Mix in the flour. Cook on Full for 30 seconds. Gradually blend in the warm milk. Cook on Full for about 4 minutes, whisking every minute, until the sauce comes to the boil and thickens. Season with salt and pepper and stir in the cheese and mustard. Cook on Full for 30 seconds or until the cheese melts. Stir in the crabmeat. Cover with a plate and reheat on Full for 2–3 minutes. Serve on freshly made toast.

Tuna Mornay

Serves 4

Prepare as for Crab Mornay, but substitute canned tuna in oil for the crabmeat. Flake up the flesh with two forks and add to the sauce with the oil from the can.

Red Salmon Mornay

Serves 4

Prepare as for Crab Mornay, but substitute canned red salmon, drained and flaked, for the crabmeat.

Seafood and Walnut Combo

Serves 4

45 ml/3 tbsp olive oil

1 onion, chopped

2 carrots, sliced

2 celery stalks, thinly sliced

1 red (bell) pepper, seeded and cut into strips

1 green (bell) pepper, seeded and cut into strips

1 small courgette (zucchini), thinly sliced

250 ml/8 fl oz/1 cup white wine

A pinch of mixed spice

300 ml/½ pt/1¼ cups fish or vegetable stock

450 g/1 lb ripe tomatoes, blanched, skinned and chopped

125 g/4 oz squid rings

400 g/14 oz plaice or lemon sole fillet, cut into squares

125 g/4 oz cooked mussels

4 large cooked prawns (shrimp)

50 g/2 oz/½ cup walnut halves or pieces

50 g/2 oz/1/3 cup sultanas (golden raisins)

A dash of sherry

Salt and freshly ground black pepper

Juice of 1 lemon

30 ml/2 tbsp chopped parsley

Heat the oil in a 2.5 litre/4½ pt/11 cup casserole dish (Dutch oven) on Full for 2 minutes. Add all the vegetables. Cook, uncovered, on Full for 5 minutes, stirring twice. Add the wine, spice, stock and tomatoes with all the fish and seafood. Cover with clingfilm (plastic wrap) and slit it twice to allow steam to escape. Cook on Full for 10 minutes. Stir in all the remaining ingredients except the parsley. Cover as before and cook on Full for 4 minutes. Uncover, sprinkle with the parsley and serve straight away.

Salmon Ring with Dill

Serves 8–10

125 g/4 oz/3½ slices loose-textured white bread
900 g/2 lb skinned fresh salmon fillet, cubed
10 ml/2 tsp bottled anchovy sauce
5–7.5 ml/1–1½ tsp salt
1 garlic clove, crushed
4 large eggs, beaten
25 g/1 oz fresh dill (dill weed)
White pepper

Lightly butter a deep 23 cm/9 in diameter dish. Crumb the bread in a food processor. Add all remaining ingredients. Pulse the machine until the mixture is just combined and the fish coarsely minced. Avoid over-mixing or the mixture will be heavy and dense. Spread smoothly into the prepared dish and push a baby jam (conserve) jar or straight-sided egg cup into the centre so that the mixture forms a ring. Cover with clingfilm (plastic wrap) and slit it twice to allow steam to escape. Cook on Full for 15 minutes, turning the dish twice. (The ring will shrink away from the side of the dish.) Allow to stand until cool, then re-cover and chill. Cut into wedges and serve. Leftovers can be used in sandwiches.

Mixed Fish Ring with Parsley

Serves 8–10

Prepare as for Salmon Ring with Dill, but substitute a mixture of skinned fresh salmon fillet, halibut and haddock for the salmon and 45 ml/3 tbsp chopped parsley for the dill.

Cod Casserole with Bacon and Tomatoes

Serves 6

30 ml/2 tbsp butter or margarine

225 g/8 oz gammon, coarsely chopped

2 onions, sliced

1 large green (bell) pepper, seeded and cut into strips

2 3 400 g/2 3 14 oz/2 large cans tomatoes

15 ml/1 tbsp mild continental mustard

45 ml/3 tbsp Cointreau or Grand Marnier

Salt and freshly ground black pepper

700 g/1½ lb skinned cod fillet, cubed

2 garlic cloves, crushed

60 ml/4 tbsp toasted brown breadcrumbs

15 ml/1 tbsp groundnut (peanut) or sunflower oil

Put the butter or margarine in a 2 litre/3½ pt/8½ cup casserole dish (Dutch oven). Heat, uncovered, on Full for 1½ minutes. Mix in the gammon, onions and pepper. Cook, uncovered, on Defrost for 10 minutes, stirring twice. Remove from the microwave. Work in the tomatoes, breaking them down with a fork, and stir in the mustard, liqueur and seasoning. Cover with clingfilm (plastic wrap) and slit it twice to allow steam to escape. Cook on Full for 6 minutes. Add the fish and garlic. Cover as before and cook on Medium for 10 minutes. Sprinkle with the breadcrumbs and trickle the oil over the top. Heat, uncovered, on Full for 1 minute.

Slimmers' Fish Pot

Serves 2

Tinged with a hottish jalapeno sauce and assertively spiced, enjoy this luxury fish feast with crusty French bread and rustic red wine.

2 onions, coarsely chopped

2 garlic cloves, crushed

15 ml/1 tbsp olive oil

400 g/14 oz/1 large can chopped tomatoes

200 ml/7 fl oz/scant 1 cup rosé wine

15 ml/1 tbsp Pernod or Ricard (pastis)

10 ml/2 tsp jalapeno sauce

2.5 ml/½ tsp hot pepper sauce

10 ml/2 tsp garam masala

1 bay leaf

2.5 ml/½ tsp dried oregano

2.5–5 ml/½–1 tsp salt

225 g/8 oz monkfish or skinned halibut, cut into strips

12 large cooked prawns (shrimp)

2 large scallops, cut into strips

30 ml/2 tbsp chopped coriander (cilantro), to garnish

Place the onions, garlic and oil in a 2 litre/3½ pt/8½ cup casserole dish (Dutch oven). Cover with a plate and cook on Full for 3 minutes. Mix in the remaining ingredients except the fish, shellfish and coriander. Cover as before and cook on Full for 6 minutes, stirring three times. Mix in the monkfish or halibut. Cover as before and cook on Defrost for 4 minutes until the fish whitens. Stir in the prawns and scallops. Cover as before and cook on Defrost for 1½ minutes. Stir round, ladle into deep plates and sprinkle each with coriander. Serve straight away.

Roast Chicken

Microwaved chicken can be succulent and attractively flavoured if it's treated with a suitable baste and left unstuffed.

1 oven-ready chicken, size as required

For the baste:
25 g/1 oz/2 tbsp butter or margarine
5 ml/1 tsp paprika
5 ml/1 tsp Worcestershire sauce
5 ml/1 tsp soy sauce
2.5 ml/½ tsp garlic salt or 5 ml/1 tsp garlic paste
5 ml/1 tsp tomato purée (paste)

Stand the washed and dried chicken in a dish big enough to hold it comfortably and also to fit the microwave. (It needn't be deep.) To make the baste, melt the butter or margarine on Full for 30–60 seconds. Stir in the remaining ingredients and spoon over the chicken. Cover with clingfilm (plastic wrap) and slit it twice to allow steam to escape. Cook on Full for 8 minutes per 450 g/1 lb, turning the dish every 5 minutes. Half-way through cooking, switch off the microwave and allow the bird to stand inside for 10 minutes, then complete the cooking. Allow to stand for a further 5 minutes. Transfer to a carving board, cover with foil and allow to stand for 5 minutes before carving.

Glazed Roast Chicken

Prepare as for Roast Chicken, but add 5 ml/1 tsp black treacle (molasses), 10 ml/2 tsp brown sugar, 5 ml/1 tsp lemon juice and 5 ml/1 tsp brown sauce to the baste. Allow an extra 30 seconds' cooking time.

Prepare as for Roast Chicken. After cooking, divide the bird into portions and put in a clean dish. Coat with bought salsa, medium to hot according to taste. Sprinkle with 225 g/8 oz/2 cups grated Cheddar cheese. Reheat, uncovered, on Defrost for about 4 minutes until the cheese melts and bubbles. Serve with canned refried beans and slices of avocado sprinkled with lemon juice.

Coronation Chicken

1 Roast Chicken

45 ml/3 tbsp white wine

30 ml/2 tbsp tomato purée (paste)

30 ml/2 tbsp mango chutney

30 ml/2 tbsp sieved (strained) apricot jam (conserve)

30 ml/2 tbsp water

Juice of ½ lemon

10 ml/2 tsp mild curry paste

10 ml/2 tsp sherry

300 ml/½ pt/1¼ cups thick mayonnaise

60 ml/4 tbsp whipped cream

225 g/8 oz/1 cup long-grain rice, boiled

Watercress

Follow the recipe for Roast Chicken, including the baste. After cooking, remove the meat from the bones and cut into bite-sized pieces. Put into a mixing bowl. Pour the wine into a dish and add the tomato purée, chutney, jam, water and lemon juice. Heat, uncovered, on Full for 1 minute. Allow to cool. Work in the curry paste, sherry and mayonnaise and fold in the cream. Combine with the chicken. Arrange a bed of rice on a large serving dish and spoon the chicken mixture over. Garnish with watercress.

Chicken Veronique

1 Roast Chicken

1 onion, finely grated

25 g/1 oz/2 tbsp butter or margarine

150 ml/¼ pt/2/3 cup crème fraîche

30 ml/2 tbsp white port or medium-dry sherry

60 ml/4 tbsp thick mayonnaise

10 ml/2 tsp made mustard

5 ml/1 tsp tomato ketchup (catsup)

1 small celery stalk, chopped

75 g/3 oz seedless green grapes

Small bunches of green or red seedless grapes, to garnish

Follow the recipe for Roast Chicken, including the baste. After cooking, remove the meat from the bones and cut into bite-sized pieces. Put into a mixing bowl. Put the onion in a small bowl with the butter or margarine and cook, uncovered, on Full for 2 minutes. In a third bowl, beat together the crème fraîche, port or sherry, mayonnaise, mustard, tomato ketchup and celery. Fold into the chicken with the cooked onion and the grapes. Spoon neatly into a serving dish and garnish with the bunches of grapes.

Chicken in Vinegar Sauce with Tarragon

Adapted from a recipe discovered in a top restaurant in Lyons, France, in the early seventies.

1 Roast Chicken
25 g/1 oz/2 tbsp butter or margarine
30 ml/2 tbsp cornflour (cornstarch)
15 ml/1 tbsp tomato purée (paste)
45 ml/3 tbsp double (heavy) cream
45 ml/3 tbsp malt vinegar
Salt and freshly ground black pepper

Follow the recipe for Roast Chicken, including the baste. Cut the cooked bird into six portions, cover with foil and keep hot on a plate. To make the sauce, pour the chicken cooking juices into a measuring jug and make up to 250 ml/8 fl oz/1 cup with hot water. Put the butter or margarine in a separate dish and heat, uncovered, on Full for 1 minute. Stir in the cornflour, tomato purée, cream and vinegar, and season to taste with salt and freshly ground black pepper. Gradually blend in the hot chicken juices. Cook, uncovered, on Full for 4–5 minutes until thickened and bubbly, whisking every minute. Pour over the chicken and serve straight away.

Prepare as for Roast Chicken, but make several slits in the uncooked chicken skin and pack with small parsley sprigs. Put 25 g/1 oz/2 tbsp garlic butter in the body cavity. Then proceed as in the recipe.

Chicken Simla

An Anglo-Indian speciality belonging to the days of the Raj.

1 Roast Chicken

15 ml/1 tbsp butter

5 ml/1 tsp finely chopped root ginger

5 ml/1 tsp garlic purée (paste)

2.5 ml/½ tsp turmeric

2.5 ml/½ tsp paprika

5 ml/1 tsp salt

300 ml/½ pt/1¼ cups whipping cream

Fried (sautéed) onion rings, home-made or bought, to garnish

Follow the recipe for Roast Chicken, including the baste. After cooking, divide the bird into six pieces and keep hot on a large plate or in a dish. Heat the butter in a 600 ml/1 pt/2½ cup dish on Full for 1 minute. Add the ginger and garlic purée. Cook, uncovered, on Full for 1½ minutes. Mix in the turmeric, paprika and salt, then the cream. Heat, uncovered, on Full for 4–5 minutes until the cream begins to bubble, whisking at least four times. Pour over the chicken and garnish with onion rings.

Spicy Chicken with Coconut and Coriander

Serves 4

A delicately spiced curry dish from southern Africa.

8 chicken portions, 1.25 kg/2¾ lb in all

45 ml/3 tbsp desiccated (shredded) coconut

1 green chilli, about 8 cm/3 in long, seeded and chopped

1 garlic clove, crushed

2 onions, grated

5 ml/1 tsp turmeric

5 ml/1 tsp ground ginger

10 ml/2 tsp mild curry powder

90 ml/6 tbsp coarsely chopped coriander (cilantro)

150 ml/¼ pt/2/3 cup canned coconut milk

125 g/4 oz/½ cup cottage cheese with chives

Salt

175 g/6 oz/¾ cup long-grain rice, boiled

Chutney, to serve

Skin the chicken. Arrange round the edge of a deep 25 cm/10 in diameter dish, pushing the pieces closely together so they fit snugly. Cover with clingfilm (plastic wrap) and slit it twice to allow steam to escape. Cook on Full for 10 minutes, turning the dish twice. Place the coconut in a bowl with all the remaining ingredients except the rice. Stir well. Uncover the chicken and coat with the coconut mixture. Cover as before and cook on Full for 10 minutes, turning the dish four times. Serve in deep plates on a mound of rice with chutney handed separately.

Spicy Rabbit

Serves 4

Prepare as for Spicy Chicken with Coconut and Coriander, but substitute eight rabbit portions for the chicken.

Spicy Turkey

Serves 4

Prepare as for Spicy Chicken with Coconut and Coriander, but substitute eight 175 g/6 oz pieces of boned turkey breast fillet for the chicken.

Chicken Bredie with Tomatoes

Serves 6

A South African stew, using the people's most popular combination of ingredients.

30 ml/2 tbsp sunflower or corn oil

3 onions, finely chopped

1 garlic clove, finely chopped

1 small green chilli, seeded and chopped

4 tomatoes, blanched, skinned and sliced

750 g/1½ lb boned chicken breasts, cut into small cubes

5 ml/1 tsp dark soft brown sugar

10 ml/2 tsp tomato purée (paste)

7.5–10 ml/1½ –2 tsp salt

Pour the oil into a deep 25 cm/10 in diameter dish. Add the onions, garlic and chilli and mix in thoroughly. Cook, uncovered, for 5 minutes. Add the remaining ingredients to the dish and make a small hollow in the centre with an egg cup so the mixture forms a ring. Cover with clingfilm (plastic wrap) and slit it twice to allow steam to escape. Cook on Full for 14 minutes, turning the dish four times. Allow to stand for 5 minutes before serving.

Chinese Red Cooked Chicken

Serves 4

A sophisticated Chinese stew, the chicken taking on a mahogany colour as it simmers in the sauce. Eat with plenty of boiled rice to absorb the salty juices.

6 Chinese dried mushrooms
8 large chicken drumsticks, 1 kg/2¼ lb in all
1 large onion, grated
60 ml/4 tbsp finely chopped preserved ginger
75 ml/5 tbsp sweet sherry
15 ml/1 tbsp black treacle (molasses)
Grated peel from 1 tangerine or similar loose-skinned citrus fruit
50 ml/2 fl oz/3½ cup soy sauce

Soak the mushrooms in hot water for 30 minutes. Drain and cut into strips. Slash the fleshy parts of the drumsticks and arrange round the edge of a deep 25 cm/10 in diameter dish with the bony ends pointing towards the centre. Cover with clingfilm (plastic wrap) and slit it twice to allow steam to escape. Cook on Full for 12 minutes, turning the dish three times. Mix together the remaining ingredients, including the mushrooms, and spoon over the chicken. Cover as before and cook on Full for 14 minutes. Allow to stand for 5 minutes before serving.

Aristocratic Chicken Wings

Serves 4

A centuries-old Chinese recipe, favoured by the élite and eaten with egg noodles.

8 Chinese dried mushrooms
6 spring onions (scallions), coarsely chopped
15 ml/1 tbsp groundnut (peanut) oil
900 g/2 lb chicken wings
225 g/8 oz canned sliced bamboo shoots
30 ml/2 tbsp cornflour (cornstarch)
45 ml/3 tbsp Chinese rice wine or medium-dry sherry
60 ml/4 tbsp soy sauce
10 ml/2 tsp finely chopped fresh root ginger

Soak the mushrooms in hot water for 30 minutes. Drain and cut into quarters. Put the onions and oil in a deep 25 cm/10 in diameter dish. Cook, uncovered, on Full for 3 minutes. Stir round. Arrange the chicken wings in the dish, leaving a small hollow in the centre. Cover with clingfilm (plastic wrap) and slit it twice to allow steam to escape. Cook on Full for 12 minutes, turning the dish three times. Uncover. Coat with the bamboo shoots and the liquid from the can and scatter the mushrooms over the top. Blend the cornflour smoothly with the rice wine or sherry. Add the remaining ingredients. Spoon over the chicken and vegetables. Cover as before and cook on Full for 10–12 minutes until the liquid is bubbling. Allow to stand for 5 minutes before serving.

Chicken Chow Mein

Serves 4

½ cucumber, peeled and cubed
275 g/10 oz/2½ cups cold cooked chicken, cut into small cubes
450 g/1 lb fresh mixed vegetables for stir-frying
30 ml/2 tbsp soy sauce
30 ml/2 tbsp medium-dry sherry
5 ml/1 tsp sesame oil
2.5 ml/½ tsp salt
Boiled Chinese noodles, to serve

Place the cucumber and chicken in a 1.75 litre/3 pt/7½ cup dish. Mix in all the remaining ingredients. Cover with a large plate and cook on Full for 10 minutes. Allow to stand for 3 minutes before serving with Chinese noodles.

Chicken Chop Suey

Serves 4

Prepare as for Chicken Chow Mein, but substitute boiled long-grain rice for the noodles.

Express Marinaded Chinese Chicken

Serves 3

Authentic tasting but fast as can be. Eat with rice or noodles and Chinese pickles.

6 chunky chicken thighs, about 750 g/1½ lb in all
125 g/4 oz/1 cup sweetcorn kernels, half thawed if frozen
1 leek, chopped
60 ml/4 tbsp bought Chinese marinade

Place the chicken in a deep bowl and add the remaining ingredients. Mix well. Cover and chill for 4 hours. Stir. Transfer to a deep 23 cm/9 in diameter dish, arranging the chicken round the edge. Cover with clingfilm (plastic wrap) and slit it twice to allow steam to escape. Cook on Full for 16 minutes, turning the dish four times. Allow to stand for 5 minutes before serving.

Serves 2–3

4 Chinese dried mushrooms

1 large onion, chopped

1 carrot, grated

15 ml/1 tbsp groundnut (peanut) oil

2 garlic cloves, crushed

225 g/8 oz/2 cups cooked chicken, cut into strips

275 g/10 oz bean sprouts

15 ml/1 tbsp soy sauce

1.5 ml/¼ tsp sesame oil

A good pinch of cayenne pepper

2.5 ml/½ tsp salt

Boiled rice or Chinese noodles, to serve

Soak the mushrooms in hot water for 30 minutes. Drain and cut into strips. Place the onion, carrot and oil in a 1.75 litre/3 pt/7½ cup dish. Cook, uncovered, on Full for 3 minutes. Stir in the remaining ingredients. Cover with clingfilm (plastic wrap) and slit it twice to allow steam to escape. Cook on Full for 5 minutes, turning the dish three times. Allow to stand for 5 minutes before serving with rice or noodles.

Chicken with Golden Dragon Sauce

Serves 4

4 large fleshy chicken joints, 225 g/8 oz each, skinned

Plain (all-purpose) flour

1 small onion, chopped

2 garlic cloves, crushed

30 ml/2 tbsp soy sauce

30 ml/2 tbsp medium-dry sherry

30 ml/2 tbsp groundnut (peanut) oil

60 ml/4 tbsp lemon juice

60 ml/4 tbsp light soft brown sugar

45 ml/3 tbsp melted and sieved (strained) apricot jam (conserve)

5 ml/1 tsp ground coriander (cilantro)

3–4 drops hot pepper sauce

Bean sprout salad and Chinese noodles, to serve

Slash the thick parts of the chicken joints in several places with a sharp knife, dust with flour, then arrange in a deep 25 cm/10 in diameter dish. Thoroughly stir together the remaining ingredients. Pour over the chicken. Cover the dish loosely with kitchen paper and leave to marinate in the refrigerator for 4–5 hours, turning the joints over twice. Arrange the slashed sides uppermost, then cover the dish with clingfilm (plastic wrap) and slit it twice to allow steam to escape. Cook on Full for 22 minutes, turning the dish four times. Serve on a bed of noodles and coat with juices from dish.

Ginger Chicken Wings with Lettuce

Serves 4–5

1 large cos (romaine) lettuce, shredded

2.5 cm/1 in piece root ginger, thinly sliced

2 garlic cloves, crushed

15 ml/1 tbsp groundnut (peanut) oil

300 ml/½ pt/1¼ cups boiling chicken stock

30 ml/2 tbsp cornflour (cornstarch)

2.5 ml/½ tsp five spice powder

60 ml/4 tbsp cold water

5 ml/1 tsp soy sauce

5 ml/1 tsp salt

1 kg/2¼ lb chicken wings

Boiled rice or Chinese noodles, to serve

Put the lettuce, ginger, garlic and oil into a fairly large casserole dish (Dutch oven). Cover with a plate and cook on Full for 5 minutes. Uncover and add the boiling stock. Blend the cornflour and five spice powder smoothly with the cold water. Stir in the soy sauce and salt. Mix into the lettuce mixture with the chicken wings, tossing gently until thoroughly combined. Cover with clingfilm (plastic wrap) and slit it twice to allow steam to escape. Cook on Full for 20 minutes, turning the dish four times. Allow to stand for 5 minutes before serving with rice or noodles.

Bangkok Coconut Chicken

Serves 4

The genuine article, made in my kitchen by a young Thai friend.

4 part-boned chicken breasts, 175 g/6 oz each

200 ml/7 fl oz/scant 1 cup creamed coconut

Juice of 1 lime

30 ml/2 tbsp cold water

2 garlic cloves, crushed

5 ml/1 tsp salt

1 stalk lemon grass, halved lengthways, or 6 lemon balm leaves

2–6 green chillies or 1.5–2.5 ml/¼–½ tsp dried red chilli powder

4–5 fresh lime leaves

20 ml/4 tsp chopped coriander (cilantro)

175 g/6 oz/¾ cup long-grain rice, boiled

Arrange the chicken round the edge of a deep 20 cm/8 in diameter dish, leaving a hollow in the centre. Cover with clingfilm (plastic wrap) and slit it twice to allow steam to escape. Cook on Full for 6 minutes, turning the dish twice. Combine the coconut cream, lime juice and water, then stir in the garlic and salt and pour over the chicken. Sprinkle on the lemon grass or lemon balm leaves, chillies to taste and lime leaves. Cover as before and cook on Full for 8 minutes, turning the dish three times. Allow to stand for 5 minutes. Uncover and stir in the coriander, then serve with the rice.

Chicken Satay

Serves 8 as a starter, 4 as a main course

For the marinade:

30 ml/2 tbsp groundnut (peanut) oil

30 ml/2 tbsp soy sauce

1 garlic clove, crushed

900 g/2 lb boned chicken breast, cubed

For the satay sauce:

10 ml/2 tsp groundnut oil

1 onion, chopped

2 green chillies, each about 8 cm/3 in long, seeded and finely chopped

2 garlic cloves, crushed

150 ml/¼ pt/2/3 cup boiling water

60 ml/4 tbsp crunchy peanut butter

10 ml/2 tsp wine vinegar

2.5 ml/½ tsp salt

175 g/6 oz/¾ cup long-grain rice, boiled (optional)

To make the marinade, combine the oil, soy sauce and garlic in a mixing bowl and add the chicken, stirring well to coat thoroughly. Cover and chill for 4 hours in winter, 8 in summer.

To make the sauce, pour the oil into a medium-sized dish or bowl and add the onion, chillies and garlic. Before completing the sauce, thread the chicken cubes on eight oiled skewers. Arrange, four at a time, on a large plate like the spokes of a wheel. Cook, uncovered, on Full for 5 minutes, turning over once. Repeat with the remaining four skewers. Keep hot. To finish the sauce, cover the bowl with clingfilm (plastic wrap) and slit it twice to allow steam to escape. Cook on Full for 2 minutes. Stir in the boiling water, peanut butter, vinegar and salt. Cook, uncovered, for 3 minutes, stirring once. Allow to stand for 30 seconds and serve, with the rice if a main course.

Peanut Chicken

Serves 4

4 boned chicken breasts, 175 g/6 oz each
125 g/4 oz/½ cup smooth peanut butter
2.5 ml/½ tsp ground ginger
2.5 ml/½ tsp garlic salt
10 ml/2 tsp mild curry powder
Chinese hoisin sauce
Boiled Chinese noodles, to serve

Arrange the chicken round the edge of a deep 23 cm/9 in diameter dish, leaving a hollow in the centre. Put the peanut butter, ginger, garlic salt and curry powder in a small dish and heat, uncovered, on Full for 1 minute. Spread evenly over the chicken, then coat lightly with hoisin sauce. Cover with clingfilm (plastic wrap) and slit it twice to allow steam to escape. Cook on Full for 16 minutes, turning the dish four times. Allow to stand for 5 minutes before serving with Chinese noodles.

Serves 4

A fuss-free curry, fast to put together. It is low in fat so recommended for slimmers, perhaps with a side dish of cauliflower and a slice or two of seedy bread.

750 g/1½ lb skinned chicken thighs

150 ml/¼ pt/2/3 cup plain yoghurt

15 ml/1 tbsp milk

5 ml/1 tsp garam masala

1.5 ml/¼ tsp turmeric

5 ml/1 tsp ground ginger

5 ml/1 tsp ground coriander (cilantro)

5 ml/1 tsp ground cumin

15 ml/1 tbsp corn or sunflower oil

45 ml/3 tbsp hot water

60 ml/4 tbsp coarsely chopped coriander, to garnish

Place the chicken in a deep 30 cm/12 in diameter dish. Beat together all the remaining ingredients and spoon over the chicken. Cover and marinate in the refrigerator for 6–8 hours. Cover with a plate and warm through on Full for 5 minutes. Stir the chicken round. Cover the dish with clingfilm (plastic wrap) and slit it twice to allow steam to escape. Cook on Full for 15 minutes, turning the dish four times. Allow to stand for 5 minutes. Uncover and sprinkle with the chopped coriander before serving.

Japanese Chicken with Eggs

Serves 4

100 ml/3½ fl oz/6½ tbsp hot chicken or beef stock
60 ml/4 tbsp medium-dry sherry
30 ml/2 tbsp teriyaki sauce
15 ml/1 tbsp light soft brown sugar
250 g/9 oz/1¼ cups cooked chicken, cut into strips
4 large eggs, beaten
175 g/6 oz/¾ cup long-grain rice, boiled

Pour the stock, sherry and teriyaki sauce into a shallow 18 cm/7 in diameter dish. Stir in the sugar. Cover with clingfilm (plastic wrap) and slit it twice to allow steam to escape. Cook on Full for 5 minutes. Uncover and stir round. Mix in the chicken and pour the eggs over the top. Cook, uncovered, on Full for 6 minutes, turning the dish three times. To serve, spoon the rice into four warmed bowls and top with the chicken and egg mixture.

Portuguese Chicken Casserole

Serves 4

25 g/1 oz/2 tbsp butter or margarine or 25 ml/1½ tbsp olive oil

2 onions, quartered

2 garlic cloves, crushed

4 chicken joints, 900 g/2 lb in all

125 g/4 oz/1 cup cooked gammon, cut into small cubes

3 tomatoes, blanched, skinned and chopped

150 ml/¼ pt/2/3 cup dry white wine

10 ml/2 tsp French mustard

7.5–10 ml/1½–2 tsp salt

Put the butter, margarine or oil into a 20 cm/8 in diameter casserole dish (Dutch oven). Heat, uncovered, on Full for 1 minute. Stir in the onions and garlic. Cook, uncovered, on Full for 3 minutes. Add the chicken. Cover with clingfilm (plastic wrap) and slit it twice to allow steam to escape. Cook on Full for 14 minutes, turning the dish twice. Mix in the remaining ingredients. Cover as before and cook on Full for 6 minutes. Allow to stand for 5 minutes before serving.

English-style Spicy Chicken Casserole

Serves 4

Prepare as for Portuguese Chicken Casserole, but substitute medium-dry cider for the wine and add 5 quartered pickled walnuts with the other ingredients. Allow an extra 1 minute cooking time.

Compromise Tandoori Chicken

Serves 8 as a starter, 4 as a main course

An Indian dish traditionally made in a clay oven or tandoor, but this microwave version is entirely acceptable.

8 chicken pieces, about 1.25 kg/2¾ lb in all
250 ml/8 fl oz/1 cup thick Greek-style plain yoghurt
30 ml/2 tbsp tandoori spice mix
10 ml/2 tsp ground coriander (cilantro)
5 ml/1 tsp paprika
5 ml/1 tsp turmeric
30 ml/2 tbsp lemon juice
2 garlic cloves, crushed
7.5 ml/1½ tsp salt
Indian bread and mixed salad, to serve

Slash the fleshy parts of the chicken in several places. Lightly whip the yoghurt with all the remaining ingredients. Arrange the chicken in a deep 25 cm/10 in diameter dish and coat with the tandoori mix. Cover loosely with kitchen paper and marinate for 6 hours in the refrigerator.

Turn over, baste with the marinade and chill for a further 3–4 hours, covered as before. Cover with clingfilm (plastic wrap) and slit it twice to allow steam to escape. Cook on Full for 20 minutes, turning the dish four times. Uncover the dish and turn the chicken. Cover again with clingfilm and cook on Full for a further 7 minutes. Allow to stand for 5 minutes before serving.

Pumpkin Cake

Serves 8

Prepare as for Carrot Cake, but substitute peeled pumpkin for the carrots, allowing a medium wedge which should yield about 175 g/6 oz seeded flesh. Substitute dark soft brown sugar for light and allspice for the mixed (apple-pie) spice.

Scandinavian Cardamom Cake

Serves 8

Cardamom is much used in Scandinavian baking and this cake is a typical example of northern hemisphere exotica. Try your local ethnic food shop if you have any trouble getting the ground cardamom.

For the cake:
175 g/6 oz/1½ cups self-raising (self-rising) flour
2.5 ml/½ tsp baking powder
75 g/3 oz/2/3 cup butter or margarine, at kitchen temperature
75 g/3 oz/2/3 cup light soft brown sugar
10 ml/2 tsp ground cardamom
1 egg
Cold milk

For the topping:
30 ml/2 tbsp flaked (slivered) almonds, toasted
30 ml/2 tbsp light soft brown sugar
5 ml/1 tsp ground cinnamon

Line a deep 16.5 cm/6½ in diameter dish with clingfilm (plastic wrap), allowing it to hang very slightly over the edge. Sift the flour and baking powder into a bowl and rub in the butter or margarine finely. Add the sugar and cardamom. Beat the egg in a measuring jug and make up to 150 ml/¼ pt/2/3 cup with milk. Stir into the dry ingredients with a fork until well mixed but avoid beating. Pour into the prepared dish. Combine the topping ingredients and sprinkle over the cake. Cover with clingfilm and slit it twice to allow steam to escape. Cook on Full for 4 minutes, turning twice. Allow to stand for 10 minutes, then carefully transfer to a wire rack by holding the clingfilm. Carefully peel away the clingfilm when the cake is cold.

Fruited Tea Bread

Makes 8 slices

225 g/8 oz/11/3 cups mixed dried fruit (fruit cake mix)
100 g/3½ oz/½ cup dark soft brown sugar
30 ml/2 tbsp cold strong black tea
100 g/4 oz/1 cup self-raising (self-rising) wholemeal flour
5 ml/1 tsp ground allspice
1 egg, at kitchen temperature, beaten
8 whole almonds, blanched
30 ml/2 tbsp golden (light corn) syrup
Butter, for spreading

Closely line the base and side of a 15 cm/6 in diameter soufflé dish with clingfilm (plastic wrap), allowing it to hang very slightly over the side. Put the fruit, sugar and tea into a bowl, cover with a plate and cook on Full for 5 minutes. Stir in the flour, allspice and egg with a fork, then transfer to the prepared dish. Arrange the almonds on top. Cover loosely with kitchen paper and cook on Defrost for 8–9 minutes until the cake is well risen and beginning to shrink away from the side of the dish. Allow to stand for 10 minutes, then transfer to a wire rack by holding the clingfilm. Warm the syrup in a cup on Defrost for 1½ minutes. Peel the clingfilm off the cake and brush the top with the warmed syrup. Serve sliced and buttered.

Victoria Sandwich Cake

Serves 8

175 g/6 oz/1½ cups self-raising (self-rising) flour
175 g/6 oz/¾ cup butter or margarine, at kitchen temperature
175 g/6 oz/¾ cup caster (superfine) sugar
3 eggs, at kitchen temperature
45 ml/3 tbsp cold milk
45 ml/3 tbsp jam (conserve)
120 ml/4 fl oz/½ cup double (heavy) or whipping cream, whipped
Icing (confectioners') sugar, sifted, for dusting

Line the bases and sides of two shallow 20 cm/8 in diameter dishes with clingfilm (plastic wrap), allowing it to hang very slightly over the edge. Sift the flour on to a plate. Cream together the butter or margarine and sugar until the mixture is light and fluffy and the consistency of whipped cream. Beat in the eggs one at a time, adding 15 ml/1 tbsp flour with each. Fold in the remaining flour alternately with the milk using a large metal spoon. Spread equally into the prepared dishes. Cover loosely with kitchen paper. Cook one at a time on Full for 4 minutes. Allow to cool to lukewarm, then invert on to a wire rack. Peel away the clingfilm and leave until completely cold. Sandwich together with the jam and whipped cream and dust the top with icing sugar before serving.

Walnut Cake

Serves 8

175 g/6 oz/1½ cups self-raising (self-rising) flour
175 g/6 oz/¾ cup butter or margarine, at kitchen temperature
5 ml/1 tsp vanilla essence (extract)
175 g/6 oz/¾ cup caster (superfine) sugar
3 eggs, at kitchen temperature
50 g/2 oz/½ cup walnuts, finely chopped
45 ml/3 tbsp cold milk
2 quantities Butter Cream Icing
16 walnut halves, to decorate

Line the bases and sides of two shallow 20 cm/8 in diameter dishes with clingfilm (plastic wrap), allowing it to hang very slightly over the edge. Sift the flour on to a plate. Cream together the butter or margarine, vanilla essence and sugar until the mixture is light and fluffy and the consistency of whipped cream. Beat in the eggs one at a time, adding 15 ml/1 tbsp flour with each. Using a large metal spoon, fold in the walnuts with the remaining flour alternately with the milk. Spread equally into the prepared dishes. Cover loosely with kitchen paper. Cook one at a time on Full for 4½ minutes. Allow to cool to lukewarm, then invert on to a wire rack. Peel away the clingfilm and leave until completely cold. Sandwich together with half the icing (frosting) and top the cake with the remainder. Arrange a border of walnut halves on the top of the cake to decorate.

Carob Cake

Serves 8

Prepare as for Victoria Sandwich Cake but substitute 25 g/1 oz/¼ cup cornflour (cornstarch) and 25 g/1 oz/¼ cup carob powder for 50 g/2 oz/½ cup of the flour. Sandwich together with cream and/or canned or fresh fruit. Add 5 ml/1 tsp vanilla essence (extract) to the creamed ingredients, if wished.

Easy Chocolate Cake

Serves 8

Prepare as for Victoria Sandwich Cake, but substitute 25 g/1 oz/¼ cup cornflour (cornstarch) and 25 g/1 oz/¼ cup cocoa (unsweetened chocolate) powder for 50 g/2 oz/½ cup of the flour. Sandwich together with cream and/or chocolate spread.

Almond Cake

Serves 8

Prepare as for Victoria Sandwich Cake, but substitute 40 g/1½ oz/3 tbsp ground almonds for the same amount of flour. Flavour the creamed ingredients with 2.5–5 ml/½–1 tsp almond essence (extract). Sandwich together with smooth apricot jam (conserve) and a thin round of marzipan (almond paste).

Victoria Sandwich Gâteau

Serves 8

Prepare as for Victoria Sandwich Cake or any of the variations.
Sandwich together with cream or Butter Cream Icing (frosting) and/or
jam (conserve), chocolate spread, peanut butter, orange or lemon curd,
orange marmalade, canned fruit filling, honey or marzipan (almond
paste). Coat the top and side with cream or Butter Cream Icing.
Decorate with fresh or preserved fruits, nuts or dragees. For an even
richer cake, halve each baked layer to make total of four layers before
filling.

Nursery Tea Sponge Cake

Makes 6 slices

75 g/3 oz/2/3 cup caster (superfine) sugar
3 eggs, at kitchen temperature
75 g/3 oz/¾ cup plain (all-purpose) flour
90 ml/6 tbsp double (heavy) or whipping cream, whipped
45 ml/3 tbsp jam (conserve)
Caster (superfine) sugar, for sprinkling

Line the base and side of a 18 cm/7 in diameter soufflé dish with clingfilm (plastic wrap), allowing it to hang very slightly over the edge. Put the sugar in a bowl and warm, uncovered, on Defrost for 30 seconds. Add the eggs and beat until the mixture froths up and thickens to the consistency of whipped cream. Gently and lightly cut and fold in the flour using a metal spoon. Do not beat or stir. When the ingredients are well combined, transfer to the prepared dish. Cover loosely with kitchen paper and cook on Full for 4 minutes. Allow to stand for 10 minutes, then transfer to a wire rack by holding the clingfilm. When cold, peel away the clingfilm. Split in half and sandwich together with the cream and jam. Sprinkle the top with caster sugar before serving.

Lemon Sponge Cake

Makes 6 slices

Prepare as for Nursery Tea Sponge Cake, but add 10 ml/2 tsp finely grated lemon peel to the warmed egg and sugar mixture immediately before adding the flour. Sandwich together with lemon curd and thick cream.

Orange Sponge Cake

Makes 6 slices

Prepare as for Nursery Tea Sponge Cake, but add 10 ml/2 tsp finely grated orange peel to the warmed egg and sugar mixture immediately before adding the flour. Sandwich together with chocolate spread and thick cream.

Espresso Coffee Cake

Serves **8**

250 g/8 oz/2 cups self-raising (self-rising) flour
15 ml/1 tbsp/2 sachets instant espresso coffee powder
125 g/4 oz/½ cup butter or margarine
125 g/4 oz/½ cup dark soft brown sugar
2 eggs, at kitchen temperature
75 ml/5 tbsp cold milk

Line the base and side of an 18 cm/7 in diameter soufflé dish with clingfilm (plastic wrap), allowing it to hang very slightly over the edge. Sift the flour and coffee powder into a bowl and rub in the butter or margarine. Add the sugar. Thoroughly beat together the eggs and milk, then mix evenly into the dry ingredients with a fork. Spoon into the prepared dish and cover loosely with kitchen paper. Cook on Full for 6½–7 minutes until the cake is well risen and just beginning to shrink away from the side of the dish. Allow to stand for 10 minutes. Transfer to a wire rack by holding the clingfilm. When completely cold, peel away the clingfilm and store the cake in an airtight container.

Orange-iced Espresso Coffee Cake

Serves 8

Make the Espresso Coffee Cake. About 2 hours before serving, make up a thick glacé icing (frosting) by mixing 175 g/6 oz/1 cup icing (confectioners') sugar with enough orange juice to form a paste-like icing. Spread over the top of the cake, then decorate with grated chocolate, chopped nuts, hundreds and thousands etc.

Espresso Coffee Cream Torte

Serves 8

Make the Espresso Coffee Cake and cut into two layers. Whip 300 ml/½ pt/1¼ cups double (heavy) cream with 60 ml/4 tbsp cold milk until thick. Sweeten with 45 ml/3 tbsp caster (superfine) sugar and flavour to taste with espresso coffee powder. Use some to sandwich the layers together, then spread the remainder thickly over the top and side of the cake. Stud the top with hazelnuts.

Raisin Cup Cakes

Makes 12

125 g/4 oz/1 cup self-raising (self-rising) flour
50 g/2 oz/¼ cup butter or margarine
50 g/2 oz/¼ cup caster (superfine) sugar
30 ml/2 tbsp raisins
1 egg
30 ml/2 tbsp cold milk
2.5 ml/½ tsp vanilla essence (extract)
Icing (confectioner's) sugar, for dusting

Sift the flour into bowl and rub in the butter or margarine finely. Add the sugar and raisins. Beat the egg with the milk and vanilla essence and stir into the dry ingredients with a fork, mixing to a soft batter without beating. Divide between 12 paper cake cases (cupcake papers) and place six at a time on the microwave turntable. Cover loosely with kitchen paper. Cook on Full for 2 minutes. Transfer to a wire rack to cool. Dust with sifted icing sugar when cold. Store in an airtight container.

Coconut Cup Cakes

Makes 12

Prepare as for Raisin Cup Cakes, but substitute 25 ml/1½ tbsp desiccated (shredded) coconut for the raisins and increase the milk to 25 ml/1½ tbsp.

Chocolate Chip Cakes

Makes 12

Prepare as for Raisin Cup Cakes, but substitute 30 ml/2 tbsp chocolate chips for the raisins.

Banana Spice Cake

Serves **8**

3 large ripe bananas
175 g/6 oz/¾ cup mixture of margarine and white cooking fat
(shortening), at kitchen temperature
175 g/6 oz/¾ cup dark soft brown sugar
10 ml/2 tsp baking powder
5 ml/1 tsp ground allspice
225 g/8 oz/2 cups malted brown flour, such as granary
1 large egg, beaten
15 ml/1 tbsp chopped pecan nuts
100 g/4 oz/2/3 cup chopped dates

Closely line the base and side of a 20 cm/8 in diameter soufflé dish with clingfilm (plastic wrap), allowing it to hang very slightly over the edge. Peel the bananas and thoroughly mash in a bowl. Beat in both fats. Mix in the sugar. Toss the baking powder and allspice with the flour. Stir into the banana mixture with the egg, nuts and dates using a fork. Spread smoothly into the prepared dish. Cover loosely with kitchen paper and cook on Full for 11 minutes, turning the dish three times. Allow to stand for 10 minutes. Transfer to a wire rack by holding the clingfilm. Cool completely, then peel away the clingfilm and store the cake in an airtight container.

Banana Spice Cake with Pineapple Icing

Serves 8

Make the Banana Spice Cake. About 2 hours before serving, cover the cake with a thick glacé icing (frosting) made by sifting 175 g/6 oz/1 cup icing (confectioners') sugar into a bowl and mixing to a paste-like icing with a few drops of pineapple juice. When set, decorate with dried banana chips.

Butter Cream Icing

Makes 225 g/8 oz/1 cup

75 g/3 oz/1/3 cup butter, at kitchen temperature
175 g/6 oz/1 cup icing (confectioners') sugar, sifted
10 ml/2 tsp cold milk
5 ml/1 tsp vanilla essence (extract)
Icing (confectioners') sugar, for dusting (optional)

Beat the butter until light, then gradually beat in the sugar until light, fluffy and doubled in volume. Mix in the milk and vanilla essence and beat the icing (frosting) until smooth and thick.

Chocolate Fudge Frosting

Makes 350 g/12 oz/1½ cups

An American-style icing (frosting) which is useful for topping any plain cake.

30 ml/2 tbsp butter or margarine
60 ml/4 tbsp milk
30 ml/2 tbsp cocoa (unsweetened chocolate) powder
5 ml/1 tsp vanilla essence (extract)
300 g/10 oz/12/3 cups icing (confectioners') sugar, sifted

Put the butter or margarine, milk, cocoa and vanilla essence in a bowl. Cook, uncovered, on Defrost for 4 minutes until hot and the fat has melted. Beat in the sifted icing sugar until the frosting is smooth and quite thick. Use straight away.

Fruited Health Wedges

Makes 8

100 g/3½ oz dried apple rings
75 g/3 oz/¾ cup self-raising (self-rising) wholemeal flour
75 g/3 oz/¾ cup oatmeal
75 g/3 oz/2/3 cup margarine
75 g/3 oz/2/3 cup dark soft brown sugar
6 California prunes, chopped

Soak the apple rings in water overnight. Closely line the base and side of a shallow 18 cm/7 in diameter dish with clingfilm (plastic wrap), allowing it to hang very slightly over the edge. Put the flour and oatmeal into a bowl, add the margarine and rub in finely with the fingertips. Mix in the sugar to make a crumbly mixture. Spread half over the base of the prepared dish. Drain and chop the apple rings. Gently press with the prunes over the oatmeal mixture. Sprinkle the rest of the oatmeal mixture evenly on top. Cook, uncovered, on Full for 5½–6 minutes. Allow to cool completely in the dish. Lift out by holding the clingfilm, then peel away the clingfilm and cut into wedges. Store in an airtight container.

Fruited Health Wedges with Apricots

Makes **8**

Prepare as for Fruited Health Wedges, but

substitute 6 dried apricots, well washed, for the prunes.

Shortbread

Makes 12 wedges

225 g/8 oz/1 cup unsalted (sweet) butter, at kitchen temperature
125 g/4 oz/½ cup caster (superfine) sugar, plus extra for sprinkling
350 g/12 oz/3 cups plain (all-purpose) flour

Grease and base line a 20 cm/8 in diameter deep dish. Cream together the butter and sugar until light and fluffy, then mix in the flour until smooth and evenly combined. Spread smoothly into the prepared dish and prick all over with a fork. Cook, uncovered, on Defrost for 20 minutes. Remove from the microwave and sprinkle with 15 ml/1 tbsp caster sugar. Cut into 12 wedges when still slightly warm. Carefully transfer to a wire rack and allow to cool completely. Store in an airtight container.

Extra Crunchy Shortbread

Makes 12 wedges

Prepare as for Shortbread, but substitute 25 g/1 oz/¼ cup semolina (cream of wheat) for 25 g/1 oz/¼ cup of the flour.

Extra Smooth Shortbread

Makes 12 wedges

Prepare as for Shortbread, but substitute 25 g/1 oz/¼ cup cornflour (cornstarch) for 25 g/1 oz/¼ cup of the flour.

Spicy Shortbread

Makes 12 wedges

Prepare as for Shortbread, but sift in 10 ml/2 tsp mixed (apple-pie) spice with the flour.

Dutch-style Shortbread

Makes 12 wedges

Prepare as for Shortbread, but substitute self-raising (self-rising) flour for the plain flour and sift 10 ml/2 tsp ground cinnamon with the flour. Before cooking, brush the top with 15–30 ml/1–2 tbsp cream, then gently press on lightly toasted flaked (slivered) almonds.

Cinnamon Balls

Makes 20

A Passover Festival speciality, a cross between a biscuit (cookie) and a cake, which seems to behave better in the microwave than it does when baked conventionally.

2 large egg whites
125 g/4 oz/½ cup caster (superfine) sugar
30 ml/2 tbsp ground cinnamon
225 g/8 oz/2 cups ground almonds
Sifted icing (confectioners') sugar

Whip the egg whites until they just begin to foam, then stir in the sugar, cinnamon and almonds. Using damp hands, roll into 20 balls. Arrange in two rings, one just inside the other, round the edge of a large flat plate. Cook, uncovered, on Full for 8 minutes, turning the plate four times. Cool to just warm, then roll in icing sugar until each one is heavily coated. Allow to cool completely and store in an airtight container.

Golden Brandy Snaps

Makes 14

Quite difficult to make conventionally, these work like a dream in the microwave.

50 g/2 oz/¼ cup butter
50 g/2 oz/1/6 cup golden (light corn) syrup
40 g/1½ oz/3 tbsp golden granulated sugar
40 g/1½ oz/1½ tbsp malted brown flour, such as granary
2.5 ml/½ tsp ground ginger
150 ml/¼ pt/2/3 cup double (heavy) or whipping cream, whipped

Put the butter in a dish and melt, uncovered, on Defrost for 2–2½ minutes. Add the syrup and sugar and stir in well. Cook, uncovered, on Full for 1 minute. Stir in the flour and ginger. Place four 5 ml/1 tsp sized spoonfuls of the mixture very well apart directly on to the microwave glass or plastic turntable. Cook on Full for 1½–1¾ minutes until the brandy snaps begin to brown and look lacy on top. Carefully lift the turntable out of the microwave and allow the biscuits (cookies) to stand for 5 minutes. Lift off each one in turn with the help of a palette knife. Roll round the handle of a large wooden spoon. Press the joins together with the fingertips and slide up to the bowl end of the spoon. Repeat with the remaining three biscuits. When they are set, remove from the handle and transfer to a wire cooling rack. Repeat until the remaining mixture is used up. Store in an airtight tin. Before eating, pipe thick cream into both ends of each brandy snap and eat the same day as they soften on standing.

Chocolate Brandy Snaps

Makes 14

Prepare as for Golden Brandy Snaps. Before filling with cream, arrange on a baking sheet and brush the uppermost surface with melted dark or white chocolate. Leave to set, then add the cream.

Bun Scones

Makes about 8

A cross between a bun and a scone, these are exceptionally light and make a delicious treat eaten while still warm, spread with butter and a choice of jam (conserve) or heather honey.

225 g/8 oz/2 cups wholemeal flour
5 ml/1 tsp cream of tartar
5 ml/1 tsp bicarbonate of soda (baking soda)
1.5 ml/¼ tsp salt
20 ml/4 tsp caster (superfine) sugar
25 g/1 oz/2 tbsp butter or margarine
150 ml/¼ pt/2/3 cup buttermilk, or substitute a mixture of half plain yoghurt and half skimmed milk if unavailable
Beaten egg, for brushing
Extra 5 ml/1 tsp sugar mixed with 2.5 ml/½ tsp ground cinnamon, for sprinkling

Sift together the flour, cream of tartar, bicarbonate of soda and salt into a bowl. Toss in the sugar and finely rub in the butter or margarine. Add the buttermilk (or substitute) and mix with a fork to form a fairly soft dough. Turn out on to a floured surface and knead quickly and lightly until smooth. Pat out evenly to 1 cm/½ in thick, then cut into rounds with a 5 cm/2 in biscuit (cookie) cutter. Re-roll the trimmings and continue cutting into rounds. Place round the edge of a buttered 25 cm/10 in flat plate. Brush with egg and sprinkle with the sugar and cinnamon mixture. Cook, uncovered, on Full for 4 minutes, turning the plate four times. Allow to stand for 4 minutes, then transfer to a wire rack. Eat while still warm.

Raisin Bun Scones

Makes about 8

Prepare as for Bun Scones, but add 15 ml/1 tbsp raisins with the sugar.

Breads

Any liquid used in yeasted breads must be lukewarm – not hot or cold. The best way to achieve the correct temperature is to mix half boiling liquid with half cold liquid. If it still feels hot when you dip in the second knuckle of your little finger, cool it down slightly before use. Over-hot liquid is more of a problem than too cold liquid as it can kill off the yeast and stop the bread rising.

Basic White Bread Dough

Makes 1 loaf

A speedy bread dough for those who enjoy baking but are short of time.

450 g/1 lb/4 cups strong plain (bread) flour
5 ml/1 tsp salt
1 sachet easy-blend dried yeast
30 ml/2 tbsp butter, margarine, white cooking fat (shortening) or lard
300 ml/½ pt/1¼ cups lukewarm water

Sift the flour and salt into a bowl. Warm, uncovered, on Defrost for 1 minute. Add the yeast and rub in the fat. Mix to a dough with the water. Knead on a floured surface until smooth, elastic and no longer sticky. Return to the cleaned and dried but now lightly greased bowl. Cover the bowl itself, not the dough, with clingfilm (plastic wrap) and slit it twice to allow steam to escape. Warm on Defrost for 1 minute. Rest in the microwave for 5 minutes. Repeat three or four times until the dough has doubled in size. Quickly re-knead, then use as in conventional recipes or in the microwave recipes below.

Basic Brown Bread Dough

Makes 1 loaf

Follow the recipe for Basic White Bread Dough, but in place of the strong bread (plain) flour use one of the following:

- half white and half wholemeal flour

- all wholemeal flour

- half malted wholemeal and half white flour

-

Basic Milk Bread Dough

Makes 1 loaf

Follow the recipe for Basic White Bread Dough, but in place of the water use one of the following:

- all skimmed milk
- half full-cream milk and half water

Bap Loaf

Makes 1 loaf

A soft crusted and pale loaf, eaten more in the north of Britain than the south.

Make up either the Basic White Bread Dough, Basic Brown Bread Dough or Basic Milk Bread Dough. Knead quickly and lightly after the first rising, then shape into a round about 5 cm/2 in thick. Stand on a greased and floured round flat plate. Cover with kitchen paper and warm on Defrost for 1 minute. Allow to rest for 4 minutes. Repeat three or four times until the dough has doubled in size. Sprinkle with white or brown flour. Cook, uncovered, on Full for 4 minutes. Cool on a wire rack.

Bap Rolls

Makes 16

Make up either the Basic White Bread Dough, Basic Brown Bread Dough or Basic Milk Bread Dough. Knead quickly and lightly after the first rising, then divide equally into 16 pieces. Shape into flattish rounds. Arrange eight baps round the edge of each of two greased and floured plates. Cover with kitchen paper and cook, one plate at a time, on Defrost for 1 minute, then rest for 4 minutes, and repeat three or four times until the rolls have doubled in size. Sprinkle with white or brown flour. Cook, uncovered, on Full for 4 minutes. Cool on a wire rack.

Hamburger Buns

Makes 12

Prepare as for Bap Rolls, but divide the dough into 12 pieces instead of 16. Put six buns round the edge of each of two plates and cook as directed.

Fruited Sweet Bap Rolls

Makes 16

Prepare as for Bap Rolls, but add 60 ml/4 tbsp raisins and 30 ml/2 tbsp caster (superfine) sugar to the dry ingredients before mixing in the liquid.

Cornish Splits

Makes 16

Prepare as for Bap Rolls, but do not sprinkle the tops with flour before cooking. Halve when cold and fill with thick cream or clotted cream and strawberry or raspberry jam (conserve). Dust the tops heavily with sifted icing (confectioners') sugar. Eat the same day.

Fancy Rolls

Makes 16

Make up either the Basic White Bread Dough, Basic Brown Bread Dough or Basic Milk Bread Dough. Knead quickly and lightly after the first rising, then divide equally into 16 pieces. Shape four pieces into round rolls and cut a slit across the top of each. Roll four pieces into ropes, each 20 cm/8 in long, and tie in a knot. Shape four pieces into baby Vienna loaves and make three diagonal slits on top of each. Divide each of the remaining four pieces into three, roll into narrow ropes and plait together. Arrange all the rolls on a greased and floured baking tray and leave in the warm until doubled in size. Brush the tops with egg and bake conventionally at 230°C/450°F/gas mark 8 for 15–20 minutes. Remove from the oven and transfer the rolls to a wire rack. Store in an airtight container when cold.

Rolls with Toppings

Makes 16

Prepare as for Fancy Rolls. After brushing the tops of the rolls with egg, sprinkle with any of the following: poppy seeds, toasted sesame seeds, fennel seeds, porridge oats, cracked wheat, grated hard cheese, coarse sea salt, flavoured seasoning salts.

Caraway Seed Bread

Makes 1 loaf

Make up the Basic Brown Bread Dough, adding 10-15 ml/2–3 tsp caraway seeds to the dry ingredients before mixing in the liquid. Knead lightly after the first rising, then shape into a ball. Put into a 450 ml/¾ pt/2 cup straight-sided greased round dish. Cover with kitchen paper and warm on Defrost for 1 minute. Allow to rest for 4 minutes. Repeat three or four times until the dough has doubled in size. Brush with beaten egg and sprinkle with coarse salt and/or extra caraway seeds. Cover with kitchen paper and cook on Full for 5 minutes, turning the dish once. Cook on Full for a further 2 minutes. Leave for 15 minutes, then carefully turn out on to a wire rack.

Rye Bread

Makes 1 loaf

Make up the Basic Brown Bread Dough, using half wholemeal and half rye flour. Bake as for Bap Loaf.

Oil Bread

Makes 1 loaf

Make up either the Basic White Bread Dough or Basic Brown Bread Dough, but substitute olive, walnut or hazelnut oil for the other fats. If the dough remains on the sticky side, work in a little extra flour. Cook as for Bap Loaf.

Italian Bread

Makes 1 loaf

Make up the Basic White Bread Dough, but substitute olive oil for the other fats and add 15 ml/1 tbsp red pesto and 10 ml/2 tsp sun-dried tomato purée (paste) to the dry ingredients before mixing in the liquid. Cook as for Bap Loaf, allowing an extra 30 seconds.

Spanish Bread

Makes 1 loaf

Make up the Basic White Bread Dough, but substitute olive oil for the other fats and add 30 ml/2 tbsp dried onions (in their dry state) and 12 chopped stuffed olives to the dry ingredients before mixing in the liquid. Cook as for Bap Loaf, allowing an extra 30 seconds.

Tikka Masala Bread

Makes 1 loaf

Make up the Basic White Bread Dough, but substitute melted ghee or corn oil for the other fats and add 15 ml/1 tbsp tikka spice blend and the seeds from 5 green cardamom pods to the dry ingredients before mixing in the liquid. Cook as for Bap Loaf, allowing an extra 30 seconds.

Fruited Malt Bread

Makes 2 loaves

450 g/1 lb/4 cups strong plain (bread) flour
10 ml/2 tsp salt
1 sachet easy-blend dried yeast
60 ml/4 tbsp mixed currants and raisins
60 ml/4 tbsp malt extract
15 ml/1 tbsp black treacle (molasses)
25 g/1 oz/2 tbsp butter or margarine
45 ml/3 tbsp lukewarm skimmed milk
150 ml/¼ pt/2/3 cup lukewarm water
Butter, for spreading

Sift the flour and salt into a bowl. Toss in the yeast and dried fruit. Put the malt extract, treacle and butter or margarine into a small basin. Melt, uncovered, on Defrost for 3 minutes. Add to the flour with the milk and enough water to make a soft but not sticky dough. Knead on a floured surface until smooth, elastic and no longer sticky. Divide into two equal pieces. Shape each to fit a greased 900 ml/1½ pt/3¾ cup round or rectangular dish. Cover the dishes, not the dough, with clingfilm (plastic wrap) and slit it twice to allow steam to escape. Warm together on Defrost for 1 minute. Allow to stand for 5 minutes. Repeat three or four times until the dough has doubled in size. Remove the clingfilm. Place the dishes side by side in the microwave and cook, uncovered, on Full for 2 minutes. Reverse the position of the dishes and cook for a further 2 minutes. Repeat once more. Allow to stand for 10 minutes. Invert on to a wire rack. Store in an airtight container when completely cold. Leave for 1 day before slicing and spreading with butter.

Irish Soda Bread

Makes 4 small loaves

*200 ml/7 fl oz/scant 1 cup buttermilk or 60 ml/4 tbsp each skimmed
milk and plain yoghurt*

75 ml/5 tbsp full-cream milk

350 g/12 oz/3 cups wholemeal flour

125 g/4 oz/1 cup plain (all-purpose) flour

10 ml/2 tsp bicarbonate of soda (baking soda)

5 ml/1 tsp cream of tartar

5 ml/1 tsp salt

50 g/2 oz/¼ cup butter, margarine or white cooking fat (shortening)

Thoroughly grease a 25 cm/10 in dinner plate. Mix together the
buttermilk or substitute and milk. Tip the wholemeal flour into a bowl
and sift in the plain flour, bicarbonate of soda, cream of tartar and salt.
Rub the fat in finely. Add the liquid in one go and stir to a soft dough
with a fork. Knead quickly with floured hands until smooth. Shape
into an 18 cm/7 in round. Transfer to the centre of the plate. Cut a
deepish cross on the top with the back of a knife, then dust lightly with
flour. Cover loosely with kitchen paper and cook on Full for 7
minutes. The bread will rise and spread. Allow to stand for 10 minutes.
Lift off the plate with the help of a fish slice and place on a wire rack.
Divide into four portions when cold. Store in an airtight container for
up to only 2 days as this type of bread is best eaten fresh.

Soda Bread with Bran

Makes 4 small loaves

Prepare as for Irish Soda Bread, but add 60 ml/4 tbsp coarse bran before mixing in the liquid.

To Freshen Stale Bread

Put the bread or rolls in a brown paper bag or place between the folds of a clean tea towel (dish cloth) or table napkin. Heat on Defrost until the bread feels slightly warm on the surface. Eat straight away and don't repeat with leftovers of the same bread.

Greek Pittas

Makes 4 loaves

Make up the Basic White Bread Dough. Divide into four equal pieces and knead each lightly into a ball. Roll into ovals, each 30 cm/12 in long down the centre. Dust lightly with flour. Dampen the edges with water. Fold each in half by bringing the top edge over the bottom. Press the edges well together to seal. Place on a greased and floured baking sheet. Bake straight away in a conventional oven at 230°C/450°F/gas mark 8 for 20–25 minutes until the loaves are well risen and a deep golden brown. Cool on a wire rack. Leave until just cold, then split open and eat with Greek-style dips and other foods.

Jellied Cherries in Port

Serves 6

750 g/1½ lb canned stoned (pitted) morello cherries in light syrup,
drained and syrup reserved
15 ml/1 tbsp powdered gelatine
45 ml/3 tbsp caster (superfine) sugar
2.5 ml/½ tsp ground cinnamon
Tawny port
Double (heavy) cream, whipped, and mixed (apple-pie) spice, to
decorate

Pour 30 ml/2 tbsp of the syrup into a large measuring jug. Stir in the gelatine and leave for 2 minutes to soften. Cover with a saucer and melt on Defrost for 2 minutes. Stir to ensure the gelatine has melted. Mix in the remaining cherry syrup, the sugar and cinnamon. Make up to 450 ml/¾ pt/2 cups with port. Cover as before and heat on Full for 2 minutes, stirring three times, until the liquid is warm and the sugar has dissolved. Transfer to a 1.25 litre/2¼ pt/5½ cup basin and allow to cool. Cover and chill until the jelly mixture is beginning to thicken and set slightly round the side of the basin. Fold in the cherries and divide between six dessert dishes. Chill until completely set. Decorate with thick cream and a dusting of mixed spice before serving.

Serves 6

Prepare as for Jellied Cherries in Port, but substitute strong dry cider for the port and 5 ml/1 tsp grated orange peel for the cinnamon.

Mulled Pineapple

Serves 8

225 g/8 oz/1 cup caster (superfine) sugar

150 ml/¼ pt/2/3 cup cold water

1 large fresh pineapple

6 whole cloves

5 cm/2 in piece cinnamon stick

1.5 ml/¼ tsp grated nutmeg

60 ml/4 tbsp medium-dry sherry

15 ml/1 tbsp dark rum

Biscuits (cookies), to serve

Put the sugar and water in a 2.5 litre/4½ pt/11 cup dish and stir well. Cover with a large inverted plate and cook on Full for 8 minutes to make a syrup. Meanwhile, peel and core the pineapple and remove the 'eyes' with the tip of a potato peeler. Cut into slices, then cut the slices into chunks. Add to the syrup with the remaining ingredients. Cover with clingfilm (plastic wrap) and slit it twice to allow steam to escape. Cook on Full for 10 minutes, turning the dish three times. Allow to stand for 8 minutes before spooning into dishes and eating with crisp, buttery biscuits.

Mulled Sharon Fruit

Serves 8

Prepare as for Mulled Pineapple, but substitute 8 quartered sharon fruit for the pineapple. After adding to the syrup with the other ingredients, cook on Full for only 5 minutes. Flavour with brandy instead of rum.

Mulled Peaches

Serves 8

Prepare as for Mulled Pineapple, but substitute 8 large halved and stoned (pitted) peaches for the pineapple. After adding to the syrup with the other ingredients, cook on Full for only 5 minutes. Flavour with an orange liqueur instead of rum.

Pink Pears

Serves 6

450 ml/¾ pt/2 cups rosé wine
75 g/3 oz/1/3 cup caster (superfine) sugar
6 dessert pears, stalks left on
30 ml/2 tbsp cornflour (cornstarch)
45 ml/3 tbsp cold water
45 ml/3 tbsp tawny port

Pour the wine into a deep dish large enough to hold all the pears on their sides in a single layer. Add the sugar and stir in well. Cook, uncovered, on Full for 3 minutes. Meanwhile, peel the pears, taking care not to lose the stalks. Arrange on their sides in the wine and sugar mixture. Cover with clingfilm (plastic wrap) and slit it twice to allow steam to escape. Cook on Full for 4 minutes. Turn the pears over with two spoons. Cover as before and cook on Full for a further 4 minutes. Allow to stand for 5 minutes. Rearrange upright in the serving dish. To thicken the sauce, mix the cornflour smoothly with the water and stir in the port. Blend into the wine mixture. Cook, uncovered, on Full for 5 minutes, stirring briskly every minute until lightly thickened and clear. Pour over the pears and serve warm or chilled.

Christmas Pudding

Makes 2 puddings, each serving 6–8

65 g/2½ oz plain (all-purpose) flour

15 ml/1 tbsp cocoa (unsweetened chocolate) powder

10 ml/2 tsp mixed (apple-pie) spice or ground allspice

5 ml/1 tsp grated orange or tangerine peel

75 g/3 oz/1½ cups fresh brown breadcrumbs

125 g/4 oz/½ cup dark soft brown sugar

450 g/1 lb/4 cups mixed dried fruit (fruit cake mix) with peel

125 g/4 oz/1 cup shredded suet (vegetarian if preferred)

2 large eggs, at kitchen temperature

15 ml/1 tbsp black treacle (molasses)

60 ml/4 tbsp Guinness

15 ml/1 tbsp milk

Thoroughly grease two 900 ml/1½ pt/3¾ cup pudding basins. Sift the flour, cocoa and spice into a large bowl. Toss in the peel, breadcrumbs, sugar, fruit and suet. In a separate bowl, beat together the eggs, treacle, Guinness and milk. Stir into the dry ingredients with a fork to make a softish mixture. Divide equally between the prepared basins. Cover each loosely with kitchen paper. Cook, one at a time, on Full for 4 minutes. Allow to stand for 3 minutes inside the microwave. Cook each pudding on Full for a further 2 minutes. Turn out of the basins when cool. When cold, wrap with a double thickness of greaseproof (waxed) paper and freeze until needed. To serve, defrost completely, cut into portions and reheat individually on plates for 50–60 seconds.

Butter Plum Pudding

Makes 2 puddings, each serving 6–8

Prepare as for Christmas Pudding, but substitute 125 g/4 oz/½ cup melted butter for the suet.

Plum Pudding with Oil

Makes 2 puddings, each serving 6–8

Prepare as for Christmas Pudding, but substitute 75 ml/5 tbsp sunflower or corn oil for the suet. Add an extra 15 ml/1 tbsp milk.

Fruit Soufflé in Glasses

Serves 6

400 g/14 oz/1 large can any fruit filling
3 eggs, separated
90 ml/6 tbsp unbeaten whipping cream

Spoon the fruit filling into a bowl and stir in the egg yolks. Beat the whites to stiff peaks and fold lightly into the fruit mixture until thoroughly combined. Spoon the mixture equally into six stemmed wine glasses (not crystal) until half-filled. Cook in pairs on Defrost for 3 minutes. The mixture should rise to the top of each glass, but will drop slightly when removed from the oven. Make a slit in top of each with a knife. Spoon 15 ml/1 tbsp of the cream on to each. It will flow down the sides of the glasses to the bases. Serve straight away.

Almost Instant Christmas Pudding

Makes 2 puddings, each serving 8

*Absolutely superb, amazingly rich-tasting, deep-toned, fruity and quick
to mature so they don't have to be made weeks ahead. Canned fruit
filling is the prime mover here and accounts for the unfailing success
of the puddings.*

225 g/8 oz/4 cups fresh white breadcrumbs
125 g/4 oz/1 cup plain (all-purpose) flour
12.5 ml/2½ tsp ground allspice
175 g/6 oz/¾ cup dark soft brown sugar
275 g/10 oz/2¼ cups finely shredded suet (vegetarian if preferred)
675 g/1½ lb/4 cups mixed dried fruit (fruit cake mix)
3 eggs, thoroughly beaten
400 g/14 oz/1 large can cherry fruit filling
30 ml/2 tbsp black treacle (molasses)
Dutch Butter Blender Cream or whipped cream, to serve.

Thoroughly grease two 900 ml/1½ pt/3¾ cup pudding basins. Place the breadcrumbs into a bowl and sift in the flour and allspice. Add the sugar, suet and dried fruit. Mix to a fairly soft mixture with the eggs, fruit filling and treacle. Divide between the prepared basins and cover each loosely with kitchen paper. Cook, one at a time, on Full for 6 minutes. Allow to stand for 5 minutes inside the microwave. Cook each pudding on Full for a further 3 minutes, turning the basin twice. Turn out of the basins when cool. When cold, wrap in greaseproof (waxed) paper and refrigerate until needed. Cut into portions and reheat as directed in the Convenience Foods table. Serve with the blender cream or whipped cream.

Ultra-fruity Christmas Pudding

Serves 8–10

An oldie from Billington's Sugar, with butter or margarine replacing sugar.

75 g/3 oz/¾ cup plain (all-purpose) flour

7.5 ml/1½ tsp ground allspice

40 g/1½ oz/¾ cup wholemeal breadcrumbs

75 g/3 oz/1/3 cup demerara sugar

75 g/3 oz/1/3 molasses sugar

125 g/4 oz/2/3 cup currants

125 g/4 oz/2/3 cup sultanas (golden raisins)

125 g/4 oz/2/3 cup dried apricots, snipped into small pieces

45 ml/3 tbsp chopped roasted hazelnuts

1 small eating (dessert) apple, peeled and grated

Finely grated peel and juice of 1 small orange

50 ml/2 fl oz/3½ tbsp cold milk

75 g/3 oz/1/3 cup butter or margarine

50 g/2 oz plain (semi-sweet) chocolate, broken into pieces

1 large egg, beaten

Brandy Sauce

Thoroughly butter a 900 ml/1½ pt/3¾ cup pudding basin. Sift the flour and spice into a large bowl. Add the breadcrumbs and sugars and toss to ensure any lumps are broken down. Mix in the dried currants, sultanas, apricots, nuts, apple and orange peel. Pour the orange juice into a jug. Add the milk, butter or margarine and the chocolate. Heat on Defrost for 2½–3 minutes until the butter and chocolate have melted. Fork into the dry ingredients with the beaten egg. Spoon into the prepared basin. Cover loosely with a round of parchment or greaseproof (waxed) paper. Cook on Full for 5 minutes, turning the basin twice. Allow to stand for 5 minutes. Cook on Full for a further 5 minutes, turning the basin twice. Allow to stand for 5 minutes before inverting on to a plate and serving with Brandy Sauce.

Plum Crumble

Serves 4

450 g/1 lb stoned (pitted) plums
125 g/4 oz/½ cup soft brown sugar
175 g/6 oz/1½ cups plain (all-purpose) wholemeal flour
125 g/4 oz/½ cup butter or margarine
75 g/3 oz/1/3 cup demerara sugar
2.5 ml/½ tsp ground allspice (optional)

Place the plums in a buttered 1 litre/1¾ pt/4¼ cup pie dish. Mix in the sugar. Tip the flour into bowl and rub in the butter or margarine finely. Add the sugar and spice and toss together. Sprinkle the mixture thickly over the fruit. Cook, uncovered, on Full for 10 minutes, turning the dish twice. Allow to stand for 5 minutes. Eat hot or warm.

Plum and Apple Crumble

Serves 4

Prepare as for Plum Crumble, but substitute 225 g/8 oz peeled and sliced apples for half the plums. Add 5 ml/1 tsp grated lemon peel to the fruit with the sugar.

Apricot Crumble

Serves 4

Prepare as for Plum Crumble, but substitute stoned (pitted) fresh apricots for the plums.

Berry Fruit Crumble with Almonds

Serves 4

Prepare as for Plum Crumble, but substitute prepared mixed berry fruits for the plums. Add 30 ml/2 tbsp toasted flaked (slivered) almonds to the crumble mixture.

Pear and Rhubarb Crumble

Serves 4

Prepare as for Plum Crumble, but substitute a mixture of peeled and chopped pears and chopped rhubarb for the plums.

Serves 4

Prepare as for Plum Crumble, but substitute a mixture of stoned (pitted) and sliced nectarines and blueberries for the plums.

Apple Betty

Serves 4–6

50 g/2 oz/¼ cup butter or margarine
125 g/4 oz/2 cups crisp breadcrumbs, bought or made from toast
175 g/6 oz/¾ cup light soft brown sugar
750 g/1½ lb cooking (tart) apples, peeled, cored and thinly sliced
30 ml/2 tbsp lemon juice
Grated zest of 1 small lemon
2.5 ml/½ tsp ground cinnamon
75 ml/5 tbsp cold water
Double (heavy) cream, whipped, or ice cream, to serve

Butter a 600 ml/1 pt/2½ cup pie dish. Melt the butter or margarine on Full for 45 seconds. Stir in the breadcrumbs and two-thirds of the sugar. Combine the apple slices, lemon juice, lemon zest, cinnamon, water and remaining sugar. Fill the prepared pie dish with alternate layers of the breadcrumb and apple mixtures, beginning and ending with breadcrumbs. Cook, uncovered, on Full for 7 minutes, turning the dish twice. Allow to stand for 5 minutes before eating with thick cream or ice cream.

Nectarine or Peach Betty

Serves 4–6

Prepare as for Apple Betty, but substitute sliced stoned (pitted) nectarines or peaches for the apples.

Serves 6

This is a fine pudding from what was once known as Arabia. The orange flower water is available from some supermarkets and pharmacies.

6 large Shredded Wheats
100 g/3½ oz/1 cup toasted pine nuts
125 g/4 oz/½ cup caster (superfine) sugar
150 ml/¼ pt/2/3 cup full-cream milk
50 g/2 oz/¼ cup butter (not margarine)
45 ml/3 tbsp orange flower water

Butter a deep 20 cm/8 in diameter dish and crumble 3 of the Shredded Wheats across the base. Combine the nuts and sugar and sprinkle evenly on top. Crush over the remaining Shredded Wheats. Heat the milk and butter in a jug, uncovered, on Full for 1½ minutes. Mix in the orange flower water. Spoon gently over the ingredients in the dish. Cook, uncovered, on Full for 6 minutes. Allow to stand for 2 minutes before serving.

Cocktail of Summer Fruits

Serves 8

225 g/8 oz/2 cups gooseberries, topped and tailed

225 g/8 oz rhubarb, chopped

30 ml/2 tbsp cold water

250 g/8 oz/1 cup caster (superfine) sugar

450 g/1 lb strawberries, sliced

125 g/4 oz raspberries

125 g/4 oz redcurrants, stalks removed

30 ml/2 tbsp Cassis or orange liqueur (optional)

Put the gooseberries and rhubarb into a deep dish with the water. Cover with clingfilm (plastic wrap) and slit it twice to allow steam to escape. Cook on Full for 6 minutes, turning the dish once. Uncover. Add the sugar and stir until dissolved. Mix in the remaining fruit. Cover when cold and chill thoroughly. Add the Cassis or liqueur, if using, just before serving.

Middle Eastern Date and Banana Compôte

Serves 6

Fresh dates, usually from Israel, are readily available in the winter.

450 g/1 lb fresh dates

450 g/1 lb bananas

Juice of ½ lemon

Juice of ½ orange

45 ml/3 tbsp orange or apricot brandy

15 ml/1 tbsp rose water

30 ml/2 tbsp demerara sugar

Sponge cake, to serve

Skin the dates and slit in half to remove the stones (pits). Place in a 1.75 litre/3 pt/7½ cup serving bowl. Peel the bananas and slice directly on to the top. Add all the remaining ingredients and toss gently to mix. Cover with clingfilm (plastic wrap) and slit it twice to allow steam to escape. Cook on Full for 6 minutes, turning the dish twice. Eat warm with sponge cake.

Mixed Dried Fruit Salad

Serves 4

225 g/8 oz mixed dried fruits such as apple rings, apricots, peaches,
pears, prunes
300 ml/½ pt/1¼ cups boiling water
50 g/2 oz/¼ cup granulated sugar
10 ml/2 tsp finely grated lemon peel
Thick plain yoghurt, to serve

Wash the fruit thoroughly and place in a 1.25 litre/2¼ pt/5½ cup bowl.
Stir in the water and sugar. Cover with a plate and leave to soak for 4
hours. Transfer to the microwave and cook on Full for about 20
minutes until the fruit is tender. Stir in the lemon peel and serve warm
with thick yoghurt.

Stodgy Apple and Blackberry Pudding

Serves 6

A little melted butter
275 g/10 oz/2¼ cups self-raising (self-rising) flour
150 g/5 oz/2/3 cup butter or margarine, at kitchen temperature
125 g/4 oz/½ cup soft brown sugar
2 eggs, beaten
400 g/14 oz/1 large can apple and blackberry fruit filling
45 ml/3 tbsp cold milk
Cream or custard, to serve

Brush a 1.25 litre/2¼ pt/5½ cup round soufflé dish with the melted butter. Sift the flour into a bowl and rub in the butter or margarine finely. Add the sugar and mix to a soft consistency with the eggs, fruit filling and milk, stirring briskly without beating. Spread evenly into the prepared dish. Cook, uncovered, on Full for 9 minutes, turning the dish three times. Allow to stand for 5 minutes. Turn out into a warmed shallow dish. Spoon on to plates to serve with cream or custard.

Lemony Bramble Pudding

Serves 4

A little melted butter
225g/8 oz/2 cups blackberries, crushed
Finely grated peel and juice of 1 lemon
225 g/8 oz/2 cups self-raising (self-rising) flour
125 g/4 oz/½ cup butter or margarine
100 g/3½ oz/scant ½ cup dark soft brown sugar
2 eggs, beaten
60 ml/4 tbsp cold milk
Cream, ice cream or lemon sorbet, to serve

Brush a deep 18 cm/7 in diameter dish with melted butter. Combine the blackberries with the lemon peel and juice and set aside. Sift the flour into a bowl. Rub in the butter and sugar. Mix to a softish consistency with the crushed fruit, eggs and milk. Spread smoothly into the prepared dish. Cook, uncovered, on Full for 7–8 minutes until the pudding has risen to the top of the dish and the top has no shiny patches. Allow to stand for 5 minutes during which time the pudding will drop slightly. Loosen edges with a knife and turn out on to a warmed plate. Eat warm with cream, ice cream or lemon sorbet.

Serves 4

Prepare as for Lemony Bramble Pudding, but substitute raspberries for the blackberries.

Apricot and Walnut Upside-down Pudding

Serves 8

For the pudding:
50 g/2 oz/¼ cup butter or margarine

50 g/2 oz/¼ cup light soft brown sugar

400 g/14 oz canned apricot halves in syrup, drained and syrup
reserved

50 g/2 oz/½ cup walnut halves

For the topping:
225 g/8 oz/2 cups self-raising (self-rising) flour

125 g/4 oz/½ cup butter or margarine

125 g/4 oz/½ cup caster (superfine) sugar

Finely grated peel of 1 orange

2 eggs

75 ml/5 tbsp cold milk

2.5–5 ml/½–1 tsp almond essence (extract)

Coffee ice cream, to serve

To make the pudding, butter the base and sides of a deep 25 cm/10 in diameter dish. Add the butter or margarine. Melt, uncovered, on Defrost for 2 minutes. Sprinkle the brown sugar over the butter so that it almost covers the base of the dish. Arrange the apricot halves attractively on top of the sugar, cut sides facing, and intersperse them with the walnut halves.

To make the topping, sift the flour into a bowl. Finely rub in the butter or margarine. Add the sugar and orange peel and toss to combine. Thoroughly beat together the remaining ingredients, then fork into the dry ingredients until evenly mixed. Spread smoothly over the fruit and nuts. Cook, uncovered, on Full for 10 minutes. Allow to stand for 5 minutes, then turn out carefully into a shallow dish. Heat the reserved syrup on Full for 25 seconds. Serve the pudding with coffee ice cream and the warm syrup.

Bananas Foster

Serves 4

From New Orleans and named after Dick Foster, who was in charge of cleaning up the city's morals in the 1950s. Or so the story goes.

25 g/1 oz/2 tbsp butter or sunflower margarine
4 bananas
45 ml/3 tbsp dark soft brown sugar
1.5 ml/¼ tsp ground cinnamon
5 ml/1 tsp finely grated orange peel
60 ml/4 tbsp dark rum
Vanilla ice cream, to serve

Place the butter in a deep 23 cm/9 in diameter dish. Melt on Defrost for 1½ minutes. Peel the bananas, halve lengthways, then cut each half into two pieces. Arrange in the dish and sprinkle with the sugar, cinnamon and orange peel. Cover with clingfilm (plastic wrap) and slit it twice to allow steam to escape. Cook on Full for 3 minutes. Allow to stand for 1 minute. Heat the rum on Defrost until just warm. Ignite the rum with a match and pour over the uncovered bananas. Serve with rich vanilla ice cream.

Mississippi Spice Pie

Serves **8**

For the flan case (pie shell):
225 g/8 oz ready-prepared shortcrust pastry (basic pie crust)
1 egg yolk

For the filling:
450 g/1 lb yellow-fleshed pink-skinned sweet potatoes, peeled and
cubed
60 ml/4 tbsp boiling water
75 g/3 oz/1/3 cup caster (superfine) sugar
10 ml/2 tsp ground allspice
3 large eggs
150 ml/¼ pt/2/3 cup cold milk
30 ml/2 tbsp melted butter
Whipped cream or vanilla ice cream, to serve

To make the flan case, roll out the pastry thinly and use to line a lightly buttered 23 cm/9 in diameter fluted flan dish. Prick well all over with a fork, especially where the side joins the base. Cook, uncovered, on Full for 6 minutes, turning the dish three times. If bulges appear, gently press down with fingers protected by oven gloves. Brush all over with the egg yolk to seal holes. Cook, uncovered, on Full for a further 1 minute. Set aside.

To make the filling, put the potatoes in a 1 litre/1¾ pt/4¼ cup dish. Add the boiling water. Cover with clingfilm (plastic wrap) and slit it twice to allow steam to escape. Cook on Full for 10 minutes, turning the dish twice. Allow to stand for 5 minutes. Drain. Put into a food processor or blender and add the remaining ingredients. Work to a smooth purée. Spread evenly in the baked pastry case. Cook, uncovered, on Defrost for 20–25 minutes until the filling has set, turning the dish four times. Cool to lukewarm. Cut into portions and serve with softly whipped cream or vanilla ice cream.

Jamaica Pudding

Serves 4–5

225 g/8 oz/2 cups self-raising (self-rising) flour
125 g/4 oz/½ cup mixture white cooking fat (shortening) and
margarine
125 g/4 oz/½ cup caster (superfine) sugar
2 large eggs, beaten
50 g/2 oz/¼ cup canned crushed pineapple with syrup
15 ml/1 tbsp coffee and chicory essence (extract) or coffee liqueur
Clotted cream, to serve

Butter a 1.75 litre/3 pt/7½ cup soufflé dish. Sift the flour into a bowl and rub in the fats finely. Mix in the sugar. Mix with a fork to a soft consistency with the eggs, pineapple with syrup and coffee essence or liqueur. Spread smoothly into the dish. Cook, uncovered, on Full for 6 minutes, turning the dish once. Invert on to a serving plate and leave to stand for 5 minutes. Return to the microwave. Cook on Full for a further 1–1½ minutes. Serve with clotted cream.

Pumpkin Pie

Serves 8

Eaten in North America on the last Thursday of every November to celebrate Thanksgiving.

For the flan case (pie shell):
225 g/8 oz ready-prepared shortcrust pastry (basic pie crust)
1 egg yolk

For the filling:
½ small pumpkin or a 1.75 kg/4 lb portion, seeded
30 ml/2 tbsp black treacle (molasses)
175 g/6 oz/¾ cup light soft brown sugar
15 ml/1 tbsp cornflour (cornstarch)
10 ml/2 tsp ground allspice
150 ml/¼ pt/2/3 cup double (heavy) cream
3 eggs, beaten
Whipped cream, to serve

To make the flan case, roll out the pastry thinly and use to line a lightly buttered 23 cm/9 in diameter fluted flan dish. Prick well all over with a fork, especially where the side joins the base. Cook, uncovered, on Full for 6 minutes, turning the dish three times. If bulges appear, gently press down with fingers protected by oven gloves. Brush all over with the egg yolk to seal holes. Cook, uncovered, on Full for a further 1 minute. Set aside.

To make the filling, put the pumpkin on a plate. Cook, uncovered, on Full for 15–18 minutes until the flesh is very soft. Spoon away from the skin and leave to cool to lukewarm. Blend until smooth with the remaining ingredients. Spoon into the pastry case still in its dish. Cook, uncovered, on Full for 20–30 minutes until the filling is set, turning the dish four times. Serve warm with whipped cream. If preferred, use 425 g/15 oz/2 cups canned pumpkin instead of fresh.

Oaten Syrup Tart

Serves 6–8

An up-to-date version of treacle tart.

For the flan case (pie shell):
225 g/8 oz ready-prepared shortcrust pastry (basic pie crust)
1 egg yolk

For the filling:
125 g/4 oz/2 cups toasted muesli with fruit and nuts
75 ml/5 tbsp golden (light corn) syrup
15 ml/1 tbsp black treacle (molasses)
Whipped cream, to serve

To make the flan case, roll out the pastry thinly and use to line a lightly buttered 23 cm/9 in diameter fluted flan dish. Prick well all over with a fork, especially where the side joins the base. Cook, uncovered, on Full for 6 minutes, turning the dish three times. If bulges appear, gently press down with fingers protected by oven gloves. Brush all over with the egg yolk to seal holes. Cook, uncovered, on Full for a further 1 minute. Set aside.

To make the filling, mix together the muesli, syrup and treacle and spoon into the baked flan case. Cook, uncovered, on Full for 3 minutes. Allow to stand for 2 minutes. Cook, uncovered, on Full for a further 1 minute. Serve with cream.

Coconut Sponge Flan

Serves 8–10

For the flan case (pie shell):
225 g/8 oz ready-prepared shortcrust pastry (basic pie crust)
1 egg yolk

For the filling:
175 g/6 oz/1½ cups self-raising (self-rising) flour
75 g/3 oz/1/3 cup butter or margarine
75 g/3 oz/1/3 cup caster (superfine) sugar
75 ml/5 tbsp desiccated (shredded) coconut
2 eggs
5 ml/1 tsp vanilla essence (extract)
60 ml/4 tbsp cold milk
30 ml/2 tbsp strawberry or blackcurrant jam (conserve)

For the icing (frosting):
225 g/8 oz/11/3 cups icing (confectioners') sugar, sifted
Orange flower water

To make the flan case, roll out the pastry thinly and use to line a lightly buttered 23 cm/9 in diameter fluted flan dish. Prick well all over with a fork, especially where the side joins the base. Cook, uncovered, on Full for 6 minutes, turning the dish three times. If bulges appear, gently press down with fingers protected by oven gloves. Brush all over with the egg yolk to seal holes. Cook, uncovered, on Full for a further 1 minute. Set aside.

To make the coconut filling, sift the flour into a mixing bowl. Rub in the butter or margarine. Toss in the sugar and coconut, then mix to a soft batter with the eggs, vanilla and milk. Spread the jam over the pastry case still in its dish. Spread evenly with the coconut mixture. Cook, uncovered, on Full for 6 minutes, turning the dish four times. The flan is ready when the top looks dry and no sticky patches remain. Allow to cool completely.

To make the icing, mix the icing sugar with enough orange flower water to make thickish icing; a few teaspoonfuls should be ample. Spread over the top of the flan. Leave until set before cutting.

Easy Bakewell Tart

Serves 8–10

Prepare as for Coconut Sponge Flan, but use raspberry jam (conserve) and substitute ground almonds for the coconut.

Crumbly Mincemeat Pie

Serves 8–10

For the flan case (pie shell):
225 g/8 oz ready-prepared shortcrust pastry (basic pie crust)
1 egg yolk

For the filling:
350 g/12 oz/1 cup mincemeat

For the nut crumble:
50 g/2 oz/¼ cup butter
125 g/4 oz/1 cup self-raising (self-rising) flour, sifted
50 g/2 oz/¼ cup demerara sugar
5 ml/1 tsp ground cinnamon
60 ml/4 tbsp finely chopped walnuts

To serve:
Whipped cream, custard or ice cream

To make the flan case, roll out the pastry thinly and use to line a lightly buttered 23 cm/9 in diameter fluted flan dish. Prick well all over with a fork, especially where the side joins the base. Cook, uncovered, on Full for 6 minutes, turning the dish three times. If bulges appear, gently press down with fingers protected by oven gloves. Brush all over with the egg yolk to seal holes. Cook, uncovered, on Full for a further 1 minute. Set aside.

To make the filling, spoon the mincemeat evenly into the baked flan case.

To make the nut crumble, rub the butter into the flour, then stir in the sugar, cinnamon and walnuts. Press over the mincemeat in an even layer. Leave uncovered and cook on Full for 4 minutes, turning the pie twice. Leave to stand for 5 minutes. Cut into wedges and serve hot with whipped cream, custard or ice cream.

Bread and Butter Pudding

Serves 4

Britain's favourite pudding.

4 large slices white bread

50 g/2 oz/¼ cup butter at kitchen temperature or soft butter spread

50 g/2 oz/1/3 cup currants

50 g/2 oz/¼ cup caster (superfine) sugar

600 ml/1 pt/2½ cups cold milk

3 eggs

30 ml/2 tbsp demerara sugar

Grated nutmeg

Leave the crusts on the bread. Spread each slice with the butter, then cut into four squares. Thoroughly butter a deep 1.75 litre/3 pt/7½ cup square or oval dish. Arrange half the bread squares over the base, buttered sides up. Sprinkle with the currants and caster sugar. Cover with the remaining bread, again buttered sides up. Pour the milk into a jug or bowl. Warm, uncovered, on Full for 3 minutes. Thoroughly beat in the eggs. Slowly and gently pour over the bread. Sprinkle with the demerara sugar and nutmeg. Allow to stand for 30 minutes, loosely covered with a piece of greaseproof (waxed) paper. Cook, uncovered, on Defrost for 30 minutes. Crisp the top under a hot grill (broiler) before serving.

Lemon Curd Bread and Butter Pudding

Serves 4

Prepare as for Bread and Butter Pudding, but spread the bread with Lemon Curd instead of butter.

Baked Egg Custard

Serves 4

Superb eaten on its own, with any kind of fruit salad combination or Cocktail of Summer Fruits.

300 ml/½ pt/1¼ cups single (light) cream or full-cream milk

3 eggs

1 egg yolk

100 g/3½ oz/scant ½ cup caster (superfine) sugar

5 ml/1 tsp vanilla essence (extract)

2.5 ml/½ tsp grated nutmeg

Thoroughly butter a 1 litre/1¾ pt/4¼ cup dish. Pour the cream or milk into a jug. Heat, uncovered, on Full for 1½ minutes. Whisk in all the remaining ingredients except the nutmeg. Strain into a dish. Stand in a second 2 litre/3½ pt/8½ cup dish. Pour boiling water into the larger dish until it reaches the level of the custard in the smaller dish. Sprinkle the top of the custard with the nutmeg. Cook, uncovered, on Full for 6–8 minutes until the custard is only just set. Remove from the microwave and allow to stand for 7 minutes. Lift the dish of custard out of the larger dish and continue to stand until the centre firms up. Serve warm or cold.

Semolina Pudding

Serves 4

Nursery food but still popular with everyone.

50 g/2 oz/1/3 cup semolina (cream of wheat)
50 g/2 oz/¼ cup caster (superfine) sugar
600 ml/1 pt/2½ cups milk
10 ml/2 tsp butter or margarine

Put the semolina in a mixing bowl. Blend in the sugar and milk. Cook, uncovered, on Full for 7–8 minutes, whisking thoroughly every minute, until boiling and thickened. Stir in the butter or margarine. Transfer to serving dishes to eat.

Ground Rice Pudding

Serves 4

Prepare as for Semolina Pudding, but substitute ground rice for the semolina (cream of wheat).

Steamed Suet Treacle Pudding

Serves 4

45 ml/3 tbsp golden (light corn) syrup
125 g/4 oz/1 cup self-raising (self-rising) flour
50 g/2 oz/½ cup shredded suet (vegetarian if preferred)
50 g/2 oz/¼ cup caster (superfine) sugar
1 egg
5 ml/1 tsp vanilla essence (extract)
90 ml/6 tbsp cold milk

Thoroughly grease a 1.25 litre/2¼ pt/5½ cup pudding basin. Pour in the syrup until it covers the base. Sift the flour into a bowl and toss in the suet and sugar. Thoroughly beat together the egg, vanilla essence and milk, then fork into the dry ingredients. Spoon into the basin. Cook, uncovered, on Full for 4–4½ minutes until the pudding has risen to reach the top of the basin. Allow to stand for 2 minutes. Turn out and spoon on to four plates. Serve with any sweet dessert sauce.

Marmalade or Honey Pudding

Serves 4

Prepare as for Steamed Suet Treacle Pudding, but substitute marmalade or honey for the syrup.

Ginger Pudding

Serves 4

Prepare as for Steamed Suet Treacle Pudding, but sift 10 ml/2 tsp ground ginger in with the flour.

Jam Sponge Pudding

Serves 4

45 ml/3 tbsp raspberry jam (conserve)
175 g/6 oz/1½ cups self-raising (self-rising) flour
75 g/3 oz/1/3 cup butter or margarine
75 g/3 oz/1/3 cup caster (superfine) sugar
2 eggs
45 ml/3 tbsp cold milk
5 ml/1 tsp vanilla essence (extract)
Whipped cream or custard, to serve

Spoon the jam into a thoroughly greased 1.5 litre/2½ pt/6 cup pudding basin. Sift the flour into a bowl. Rub in the butter or margarine finely, then toss in the sugar. Thoroughly beat together the eggs, milk and vanilla essence, then fork into the dry ingredients. Spoon into the basin. Cook on Full for 7–8 minutes until the pudding has risen to the top of the basin. Allow to stand for 3 minutes. Turn out and spoon portions on to four plates. Serve with cream or custard.

Serves 4

Prepare as for Jam Sponge Pudding, but substitute lemon curd for the jam (conserve) and add the finely grated peel of 1 small lemon to the dry ingredients.

Crêpes Suzette

Serves 4

Back in fashion after a long spell in the shadows.

8 conventionally cooked pancakes, each about 20 cm/8 in diameter
45 ml/3 tbsp butter
30 ml/2 tbsp caster (superfine) sugar
5 ml/1 tsp grated orange peel
5 ml/1 tsp grated lemon peel
Juice of 2 large oranges
30 ml/2 tbsp Grand Marnier
30 ml/2 tbsp brandy

Fold each pancake in four so that it looks like an envelope. Leave aside. Put the butter in a shallow 25 cm/10 in diameter dish. Melt on Defrost for 1½–2 minutes. Add all the remaining ingredients except the brandy and stir well. Heat on Full for 2–2½ minutes. Stir round. Add the pancakes in a single layer and baste with the butter sauce. Cook, uncovered, on Full for 3–4 minutes. Remove from the microwave. Pour the brandy into a cup and heat on Full for 15–20 seconds until tepid. Tip into a ladle and ignite with a match. Pour over the crêpes and serve when the flames have died down.

For 1 apple: score a line round a large cooking (tart) apple with a sharp knife, about one-third down from the top. Remove the core with a potato peeler or apple corer, taking care not to cut through the base of the apple. Fill with sugar, dried fruit, jam (conserve) or lemon curd. Place in a dish and cook, uncovered, on Full for 3–4 minutes, turning the dish twice, until the apple has puffed up like a soufflé. Allow to stand for 2 minutes before eating.

For 2 apples: as for 1 apple, but arrange the apples side by side on the dish and cook on Full for 5 minutes.

For 3 apples: as for 1 apple, but arrange in a triangle in the dish and cook on Full for 7 minutes.

For 4 apples: as for 1 apple, but arrange in a square in the dish and cook on Full for 8–10 minutes.

Thousand Petal Haddock with Crab

1 haddock steak or a piece of skinned fillet, about 200 g/7 oz, washed
and dried

45 ml/3 tbsp dressed crab

2.5 cm/1 in piece fresh root ginger, chopped

1 spring onion (scallion), chopped

1 garlic clove, crushed

25 ml/1½ tbsp thick mayonnaise

2.5 ml/½ tsp soy sauce

2.5 ml/½ tsp chilli sauce

5 ml/1 tsp malt vinegar

Put the fish on a dinner plate. Tip the crab into a small basin with the ginger, onion and garlic. Work in the remaining ingredients and mix thoroughly. Spread over the fish with a knife. Cover with clingfilm (plastic wrap) and slit it twice to allow steam to escape. Cook on Defrost for 8½ minutes. Allow to stand for 1½ minutes before eating.

Lemon and Thyme Cod

A mild herb dressing complements the fish brilliantly. Use hake or haddock if preferred.

1 cod steak, about 200 g/7 oz, washed and dried

10 ml/2 tsp butter or margarine

30 ml/2 tbsp single (light) cream

30 ml/2 tbsp dry lemon and thyme stuffing mix

Paprika

30 ml/2 tbsp chopped parsley

Put the fish into a shallow round dish. Melt the butter or margarine on Defrost for about 30 seconds. Mix in the cream and pour round the fish. Sprinkle the stuffing mix over the top and dust with paprika for extra colour. Cover with clingfilm (plastic wrap) and slit it twice to allow steam to escape. Cook on Defrost for 6–7 minutes. Allow to stand for 1½ minutes. Scatter the parsley over the fish before eating.

*A classic, also known as bonne femme. In culinary terms this means
anything cooked with onions, mushrooms and unsmoked bacon.*

30 ml/2 tbsp butter or margarine

1 small onion, roughly chopped

4 closed-cap mushrooms, trimmed and sliced

2 rashers (slices) lean unsmoked bacon, cut into strips

1 large cod steak, about 225 g/8 oz

Chopped parsley, to garnish

Put the butter or margarine in a 600 ml/1 pt/2½ cup round shallow
dish. Melt, uncovered, on Defrost for 1½ minutes. Mix in the onion,
mushrooms and bacon. Cover with clingfilm (plastic wrap) and slit it
twice to allow steam to escape. Cook on Full for 2 minutes. Stir round,
then place the fish on top. Cover as before and cook on Full for 4½–5
minutes. Allow to stand for 1 minute. Uncover and sprinkle with
parsley. Eat straight away.

French-style Cod

225 g/8 oz cod fillet, cut from the thicker end

50 g/2 oz mushrooms, sliced

15 ml/1 tbsp butter or margarine

1 garlic clove, crushed

5 ml/1 tsp French mustard

15 ml/1 tbsp dry white wine or calvados

Salt

Put the cod on a plate and sprinkle with the mushrooms. Place the remaining ingredients in a small dish, adding salt to taste, and heat, uncovered, on Defrost for 1½ minutes. Spoon over the fish and mushrooms. Cover with clingfilm (plastic wrap) and slit it twice to allow steam to escape. Cook on Full for 4 minutes. Allow to stand for 1 minute before eating.

Manhattan Cod

1 large cod steak, about 225 g/8 oz

50 g/2 oz cream cheese with garlic and herbs

25 g/1 oz/¼ cup strong Cheddar cheese, grated

15 ml/1 tbsp tomato ketchup (catsup)

15 ml/1 tbsp crushed cornflakes or potato crisps (chips)

Put the fish in a shallow 600 ml/1 pt/2½ cup round dish. Spread with the cream cheese and sprinkle with the Cheddar cheese. Trickle the ketchup over the top. Cover with clingfilm (plastic wrap) and slit it twice to allow steam to escape. Cook on Full for 5 minutes. Allow to stand for 1 minute. Uncover and sprinkle with the cornflakes or crisps. Eat straight away.

Curried Cod with Coconut

225 g/8 oz skinned cod fillet, cut from the thicker end

15 ml/1 tbsp butter or margarine, at kitchen temperature

2.5 ml/½ tsp mild curry powder

15 ml/1 tbsp fine desiccated (shredded) coconut

15 ml/1 tbsp single (light) cream

Salt and freshly ground black pepper

Paprika

Chopped coriander (cilantro) leaves, to garnish

Put the cod on a plate and leave aside. Put the butter or margarine, curry powder, coconut and cream in a small bowl and beat well together. Heat, uncovered, on Defrost for 1 minute. Spoon over the cod and sprinkle over salt and pepper to taste. Dust with paprika. Cover with clingfilm (plastic wrap) and slit it twice to allow steam to escape. Cook on Full for 4 minutes. Allow to stand for 1 minute. Uncover and sprinkle with coriander. Eat straight away.

Fish Vinaigrette

225 g/8 oz skinned cod or haddock fillet, cut from the thicker end
30 ml/2 tbsp bought garlic and herb vinaigrette
6 fresh tarragon or basil leaves or watercress sprigs

Put the fish on a plate and coat with the vinaigrette. Top with the herb leaves or watercress sprigs. Cover with clingfilm (plastic wrap) and slit it twice to allow steam to escape. Cook on Full for 4 minutes. Allow to stand for 1 minute before eating.

Jugged Kipper

Imagine... A kipper with no lingering smell! Once upon a time kippers were cooked by being left in a jug of hot water but this microwave method also does an immaculate and similar job.

1 medium kipper fillet, thawed if frozen
Butter or margarine

Place the kipper in a shallow 20 cm/8 in square dish. Add just enough cold water to cover the fish. Cover with clingfilm (plastic wrap) and slit it twice to allow steam to escape. Cook on Full for 6 minutes. Allow to stand for 2 minutes. Uncover and drain. Serve topped with a knob of butter or margarine.